This book belongs to

———————————

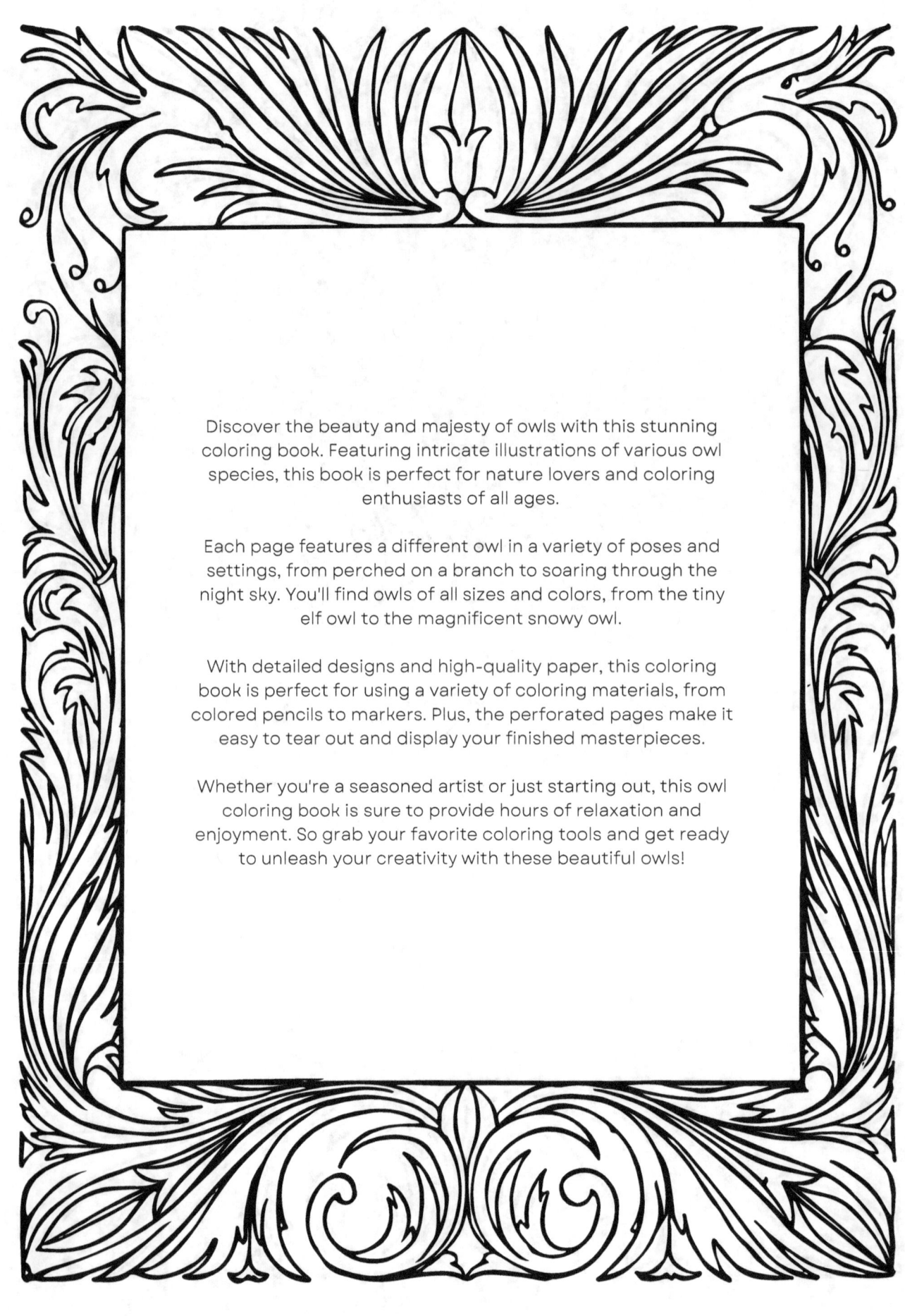

Discover the beauty and majesty of owls with this stunning coloring book. Featuring intricate illustrations of various owl species, this book is perfect for nature lovers and coloring enthusiasts of all ages.

Each page features a different owl in a variety of poses and settings, from perched on a branch to soaring through the night sky. You'll find owls of all sizes and colors, from the tiny elf owl to the magnificent snowy owl.

With detailed designs and high-quality paper, this coloring book is perfect for using a variety of coloring materials, from colored pencils to markers. Plus, the perforated pages make it easy to tear out and display your finished masterpieces.

Whether you're a seasoned artist or just starting out, this owl coloring book is sure to provide hours of relaxation and enjoyment. So grab your favorite coloring tools and get ready to unleash your creativity with these beautiful owls!

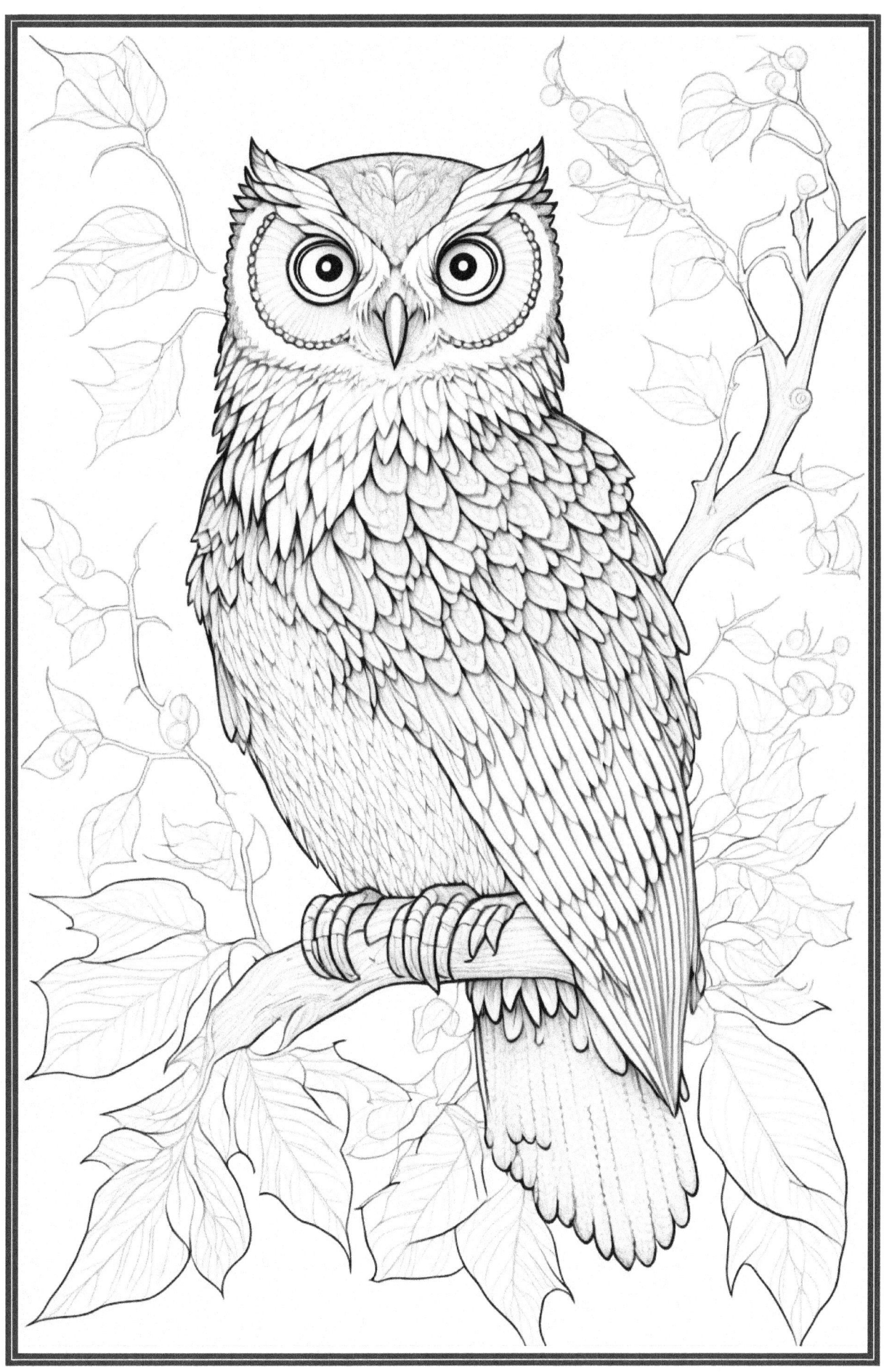

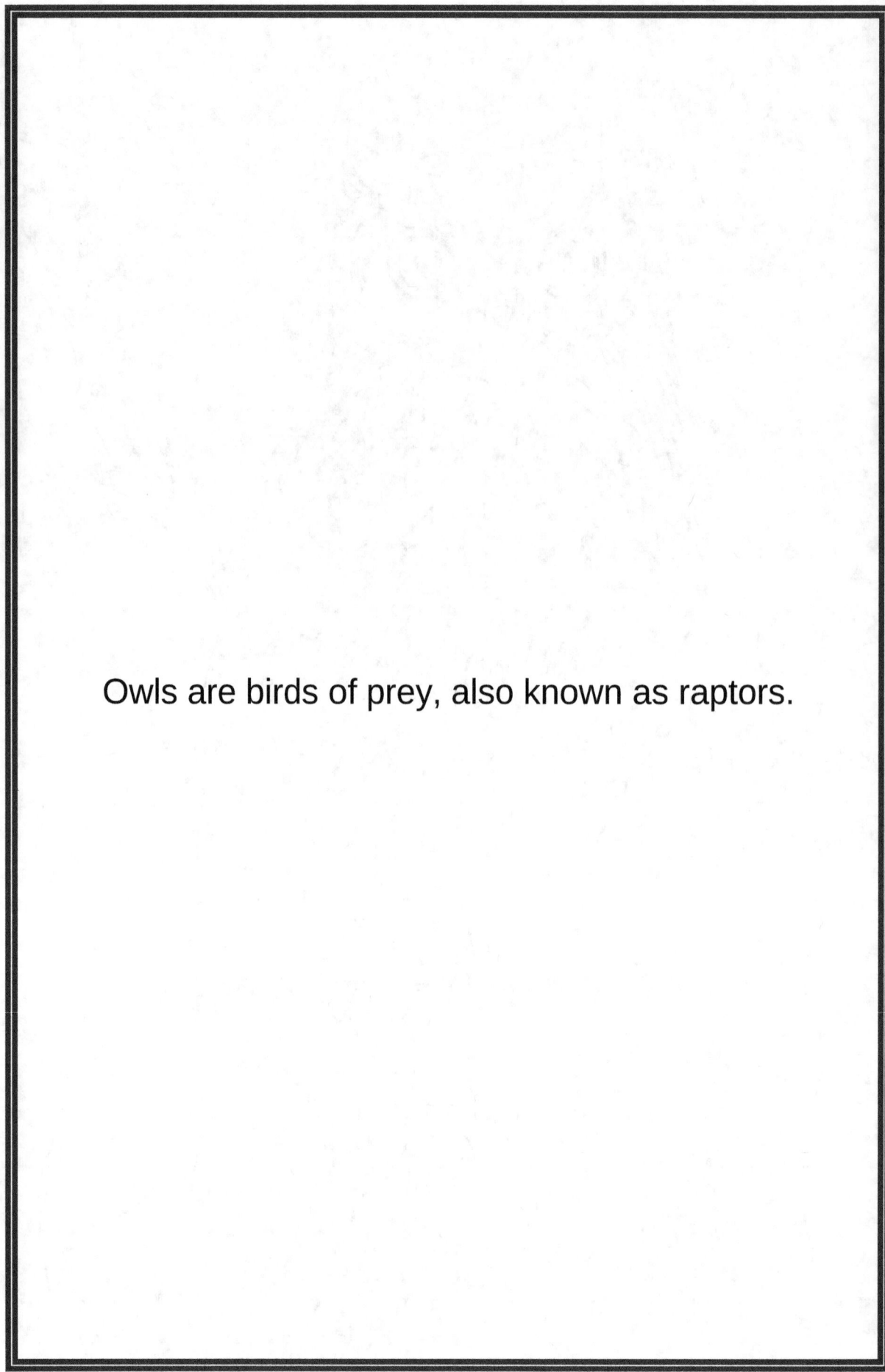

Owls are birds of prey, also known as raptors.

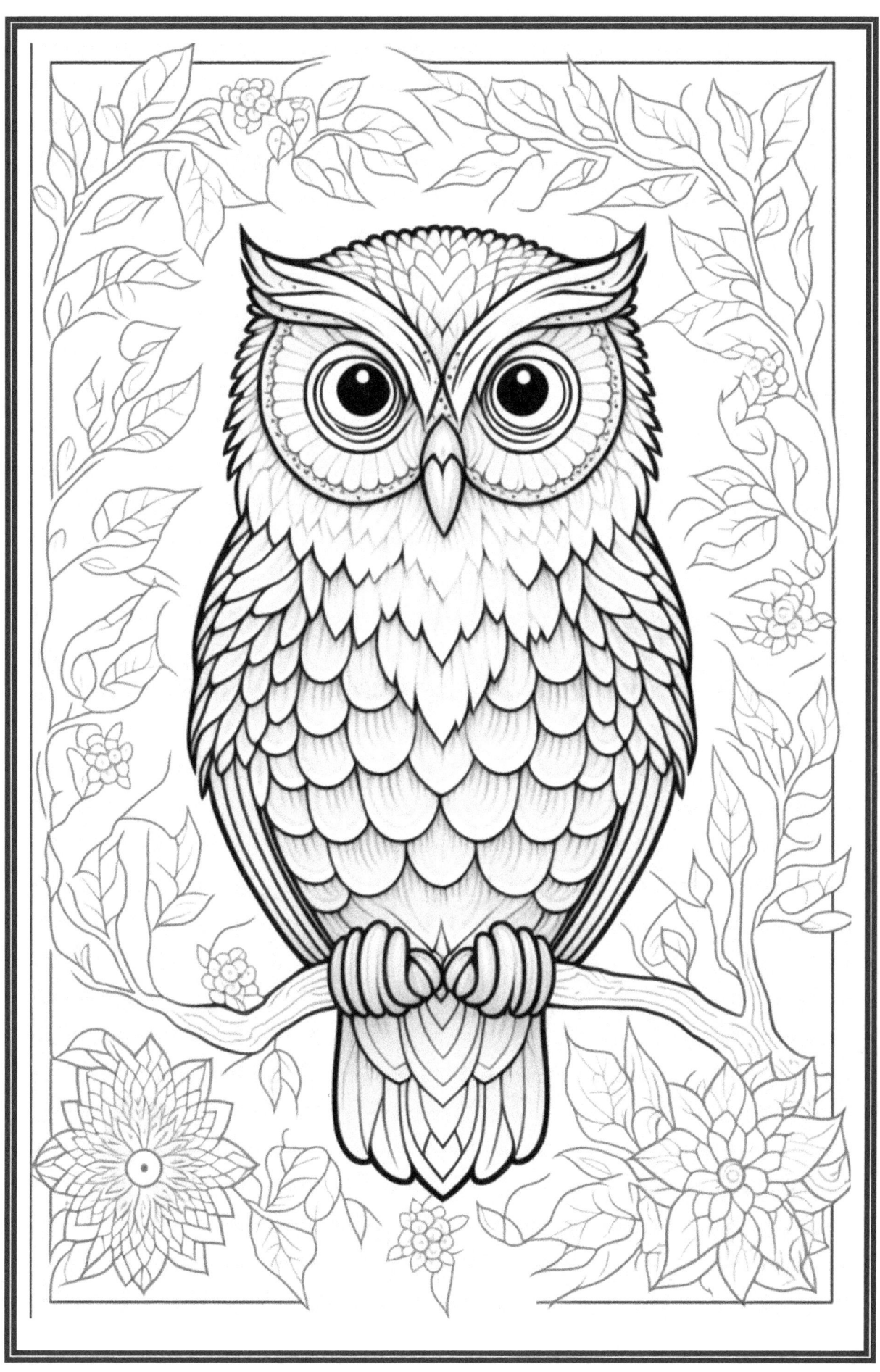

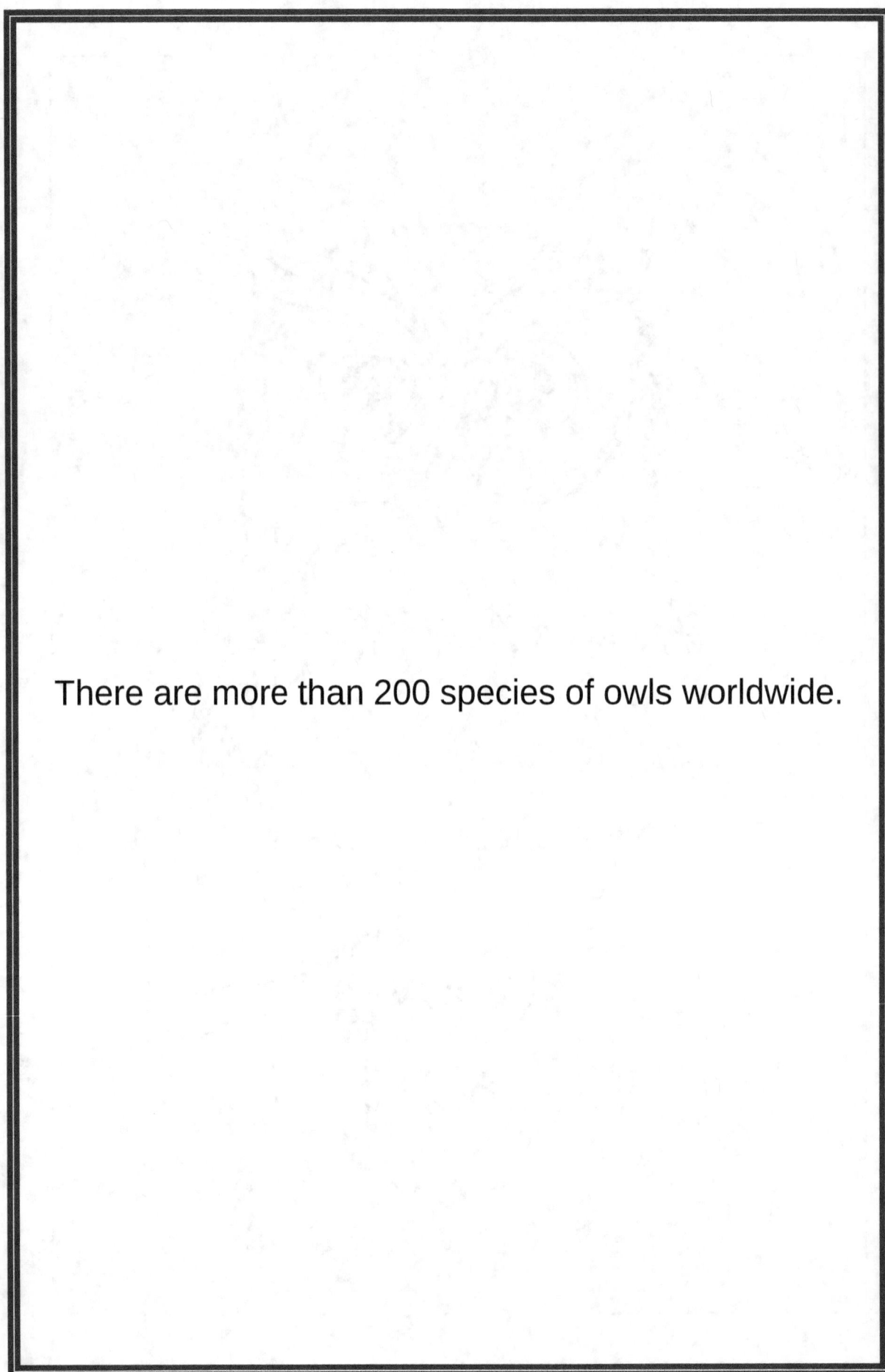

There are more than 200 species of owls worldwide.

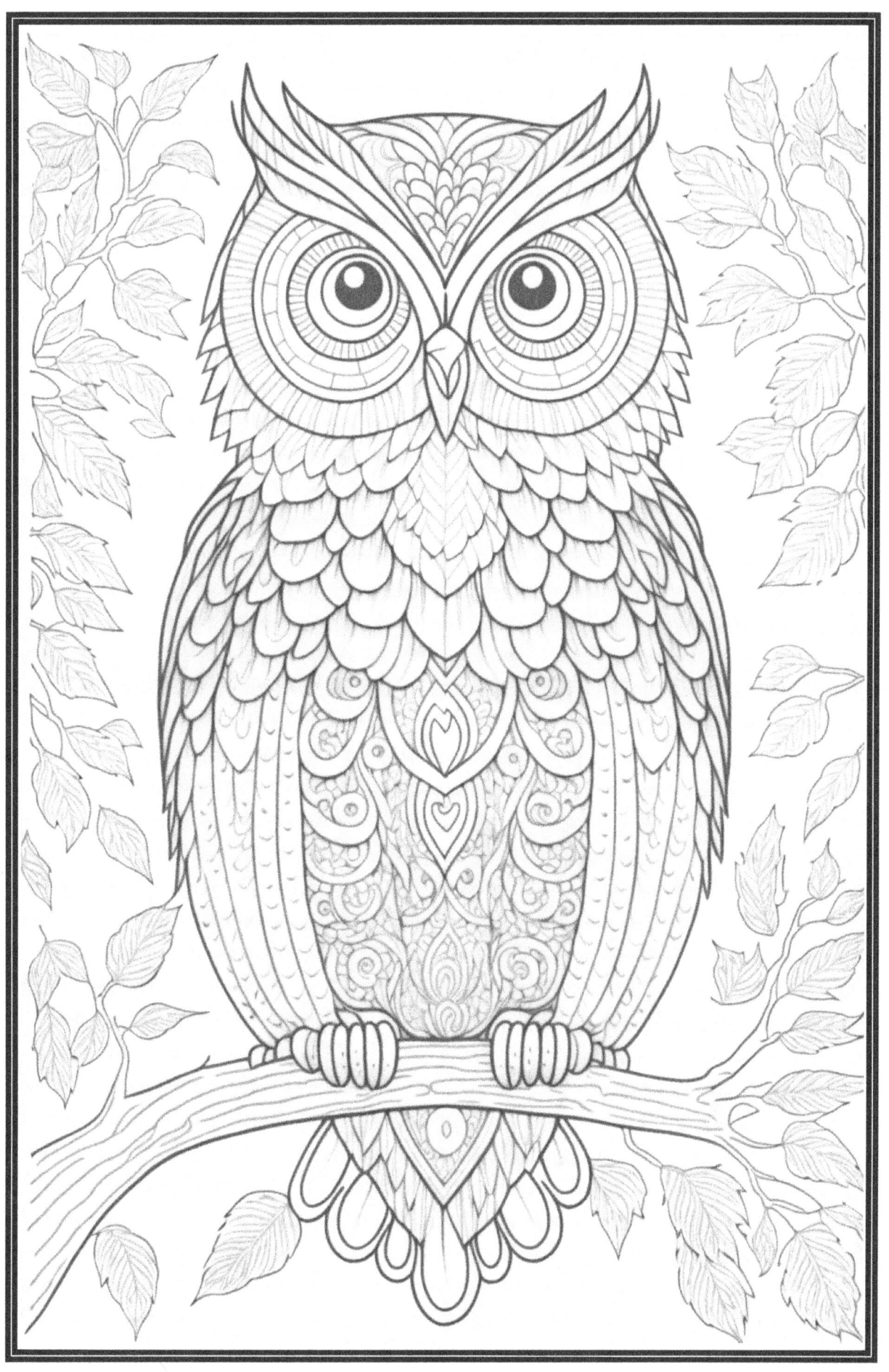

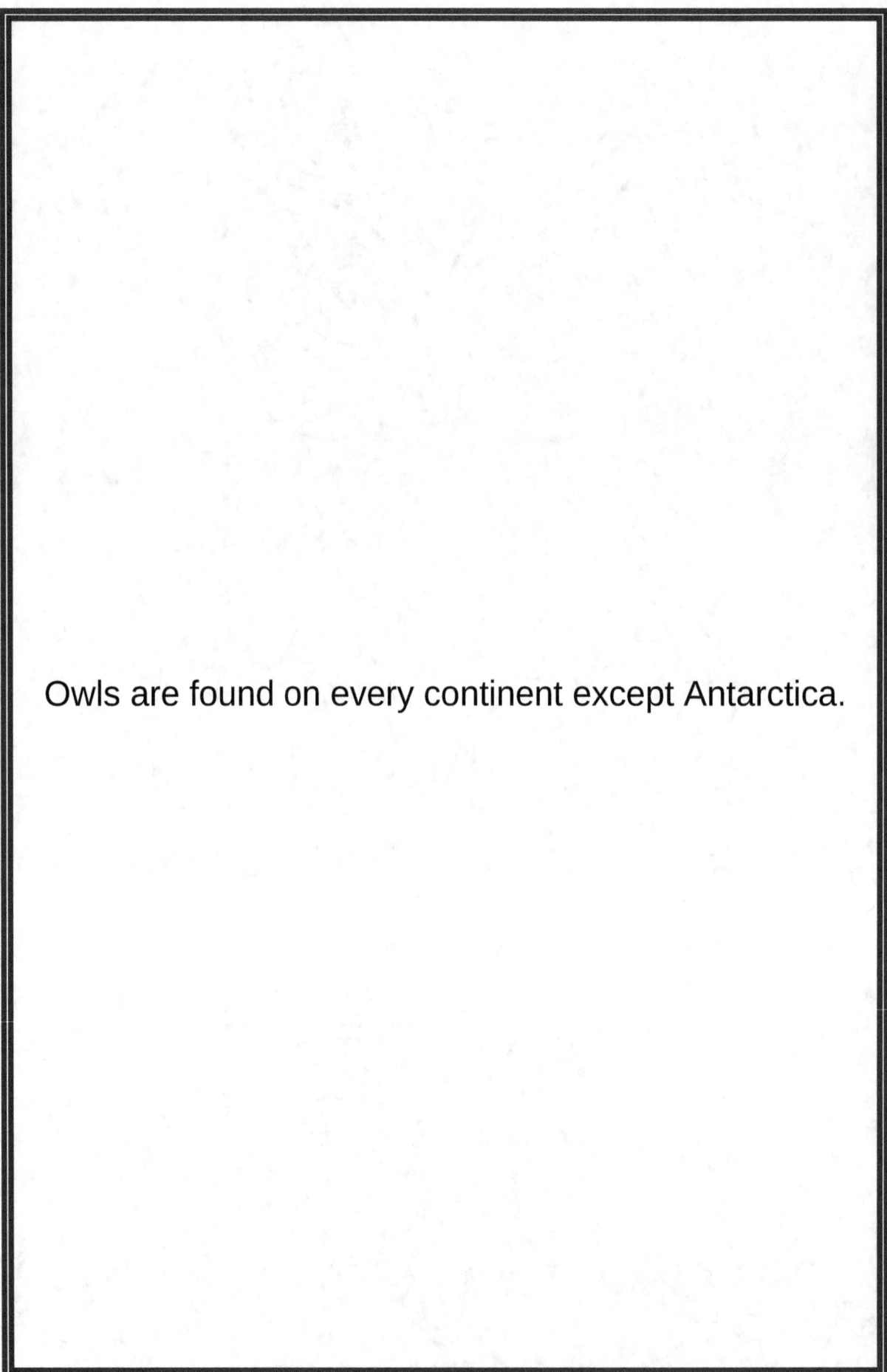

Owls are found on every continent except Antarctica.

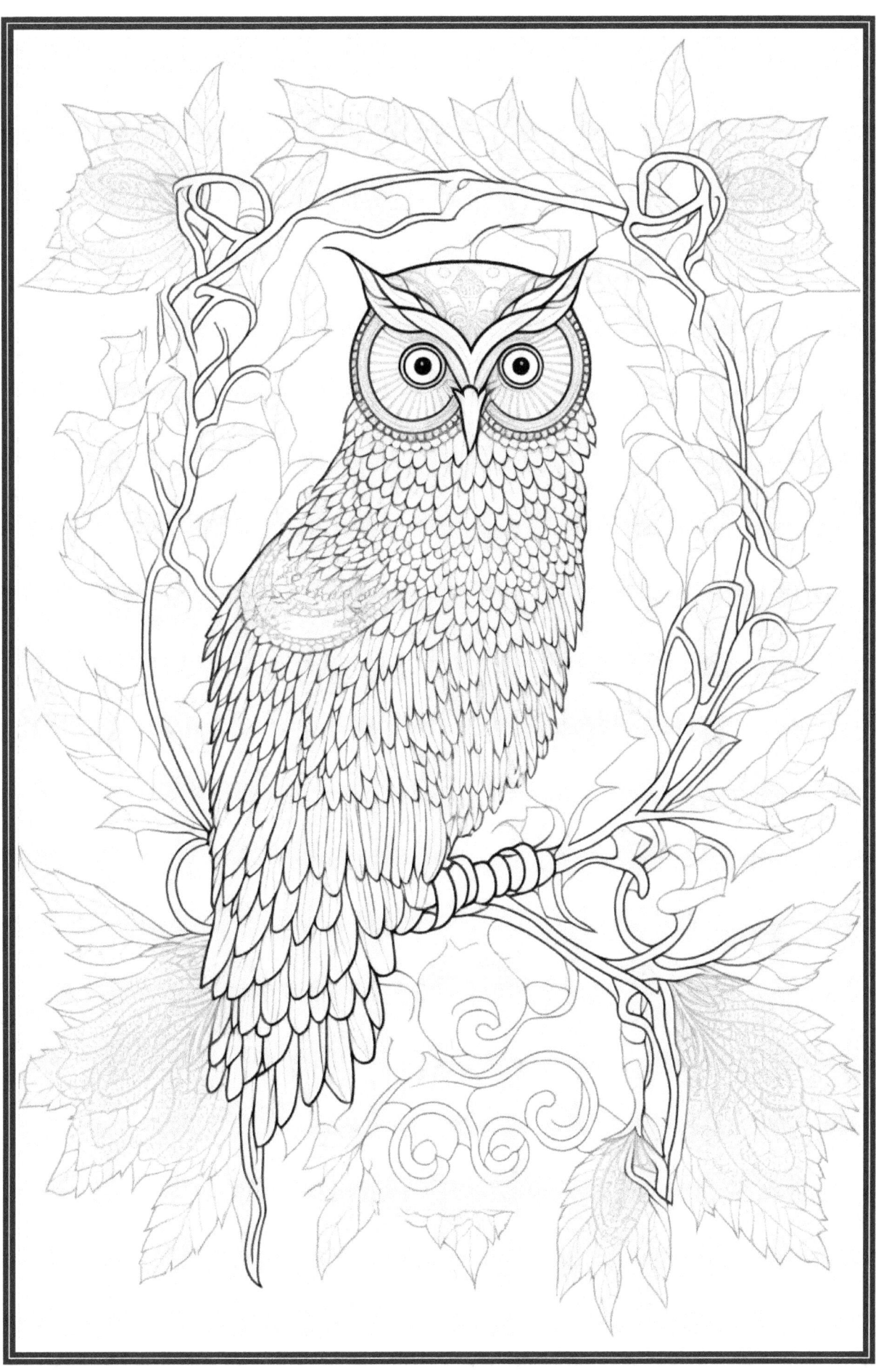

Owls have big, forward-facing eyes that give them binocular vision.

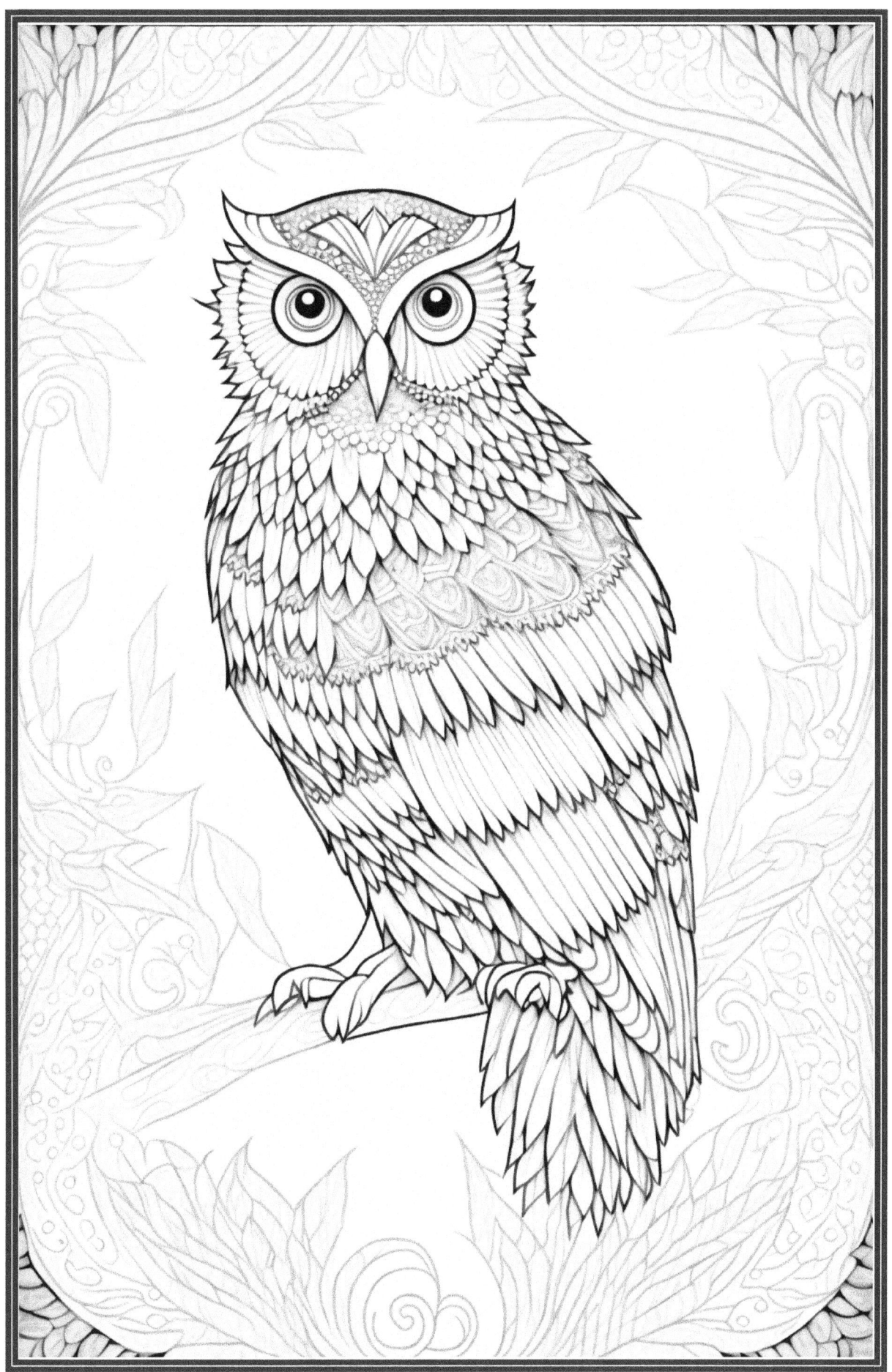

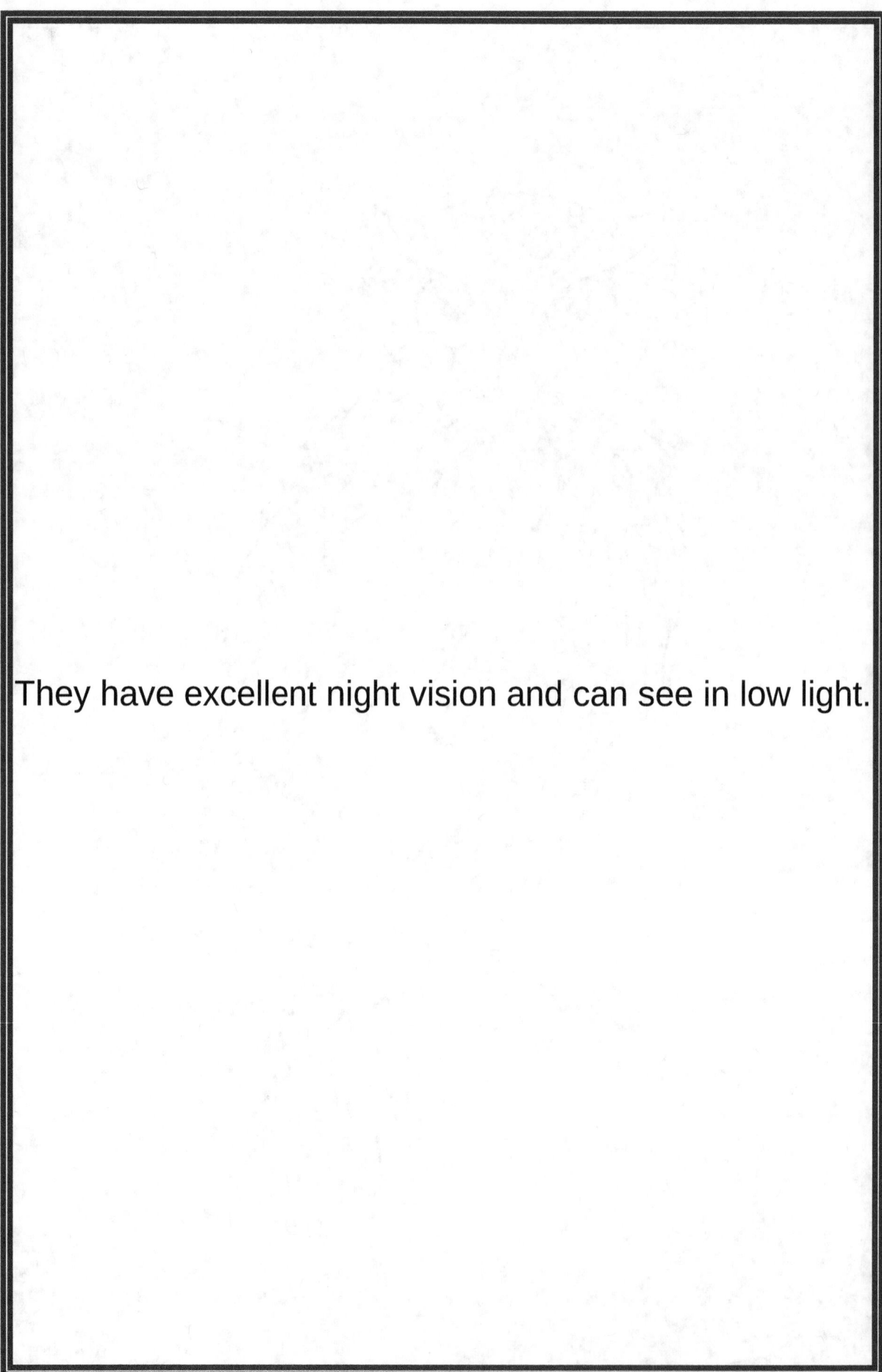

They have excellent night vision and can see in low light.

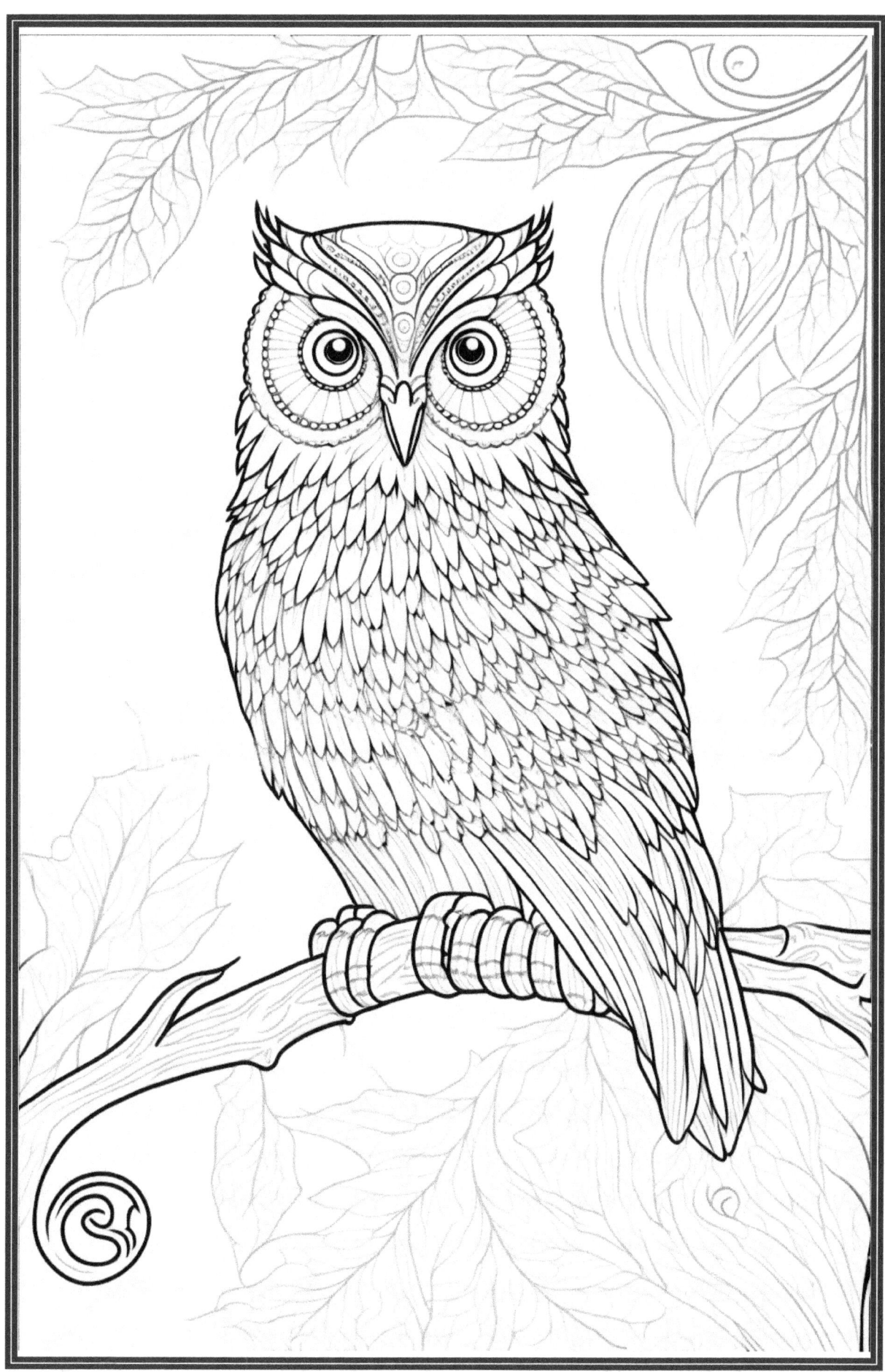

Owls have feathered facial disks that help to focus sound waves onto their ears.

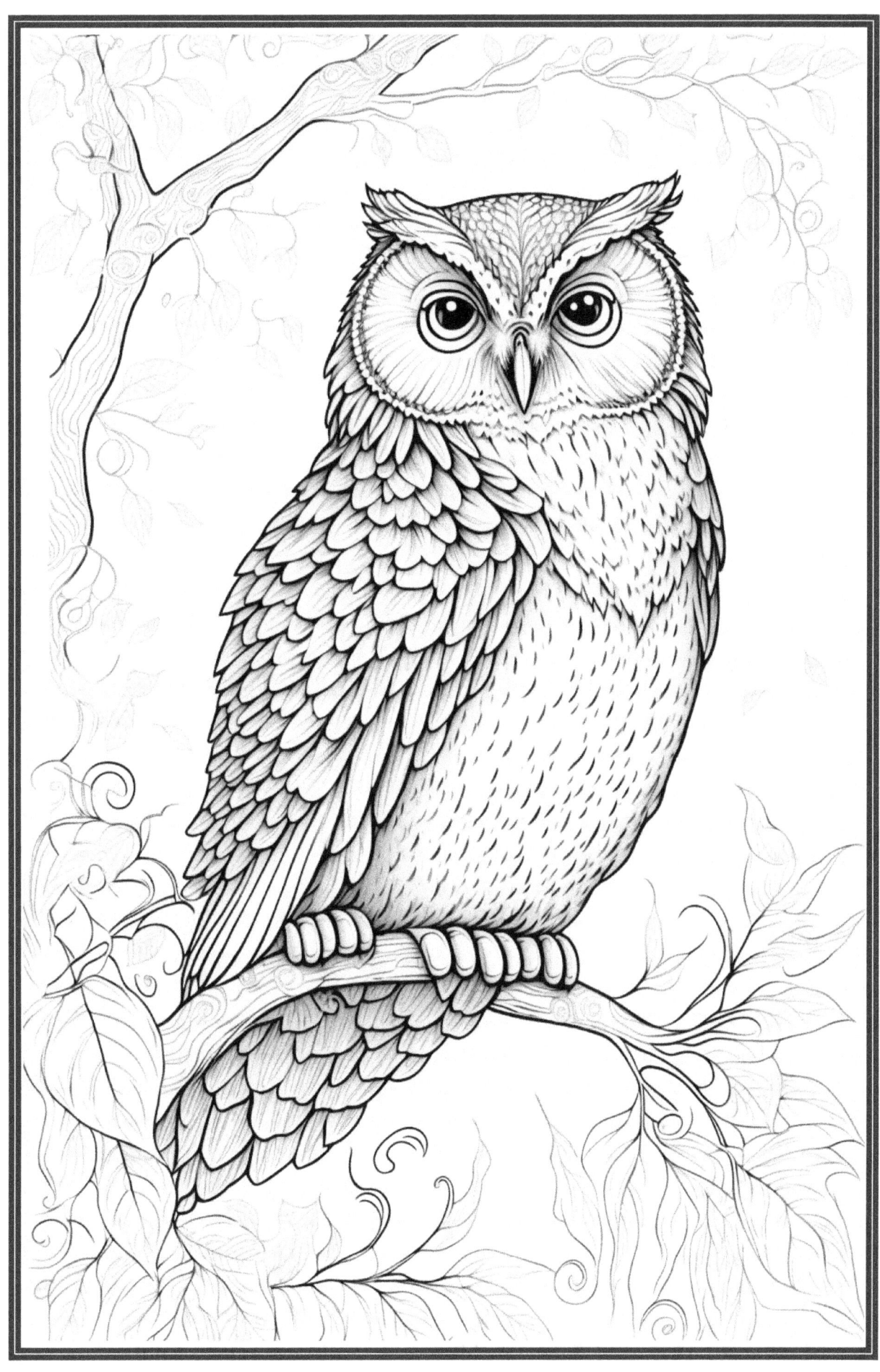

They can turn their heads up to 270 degrees.

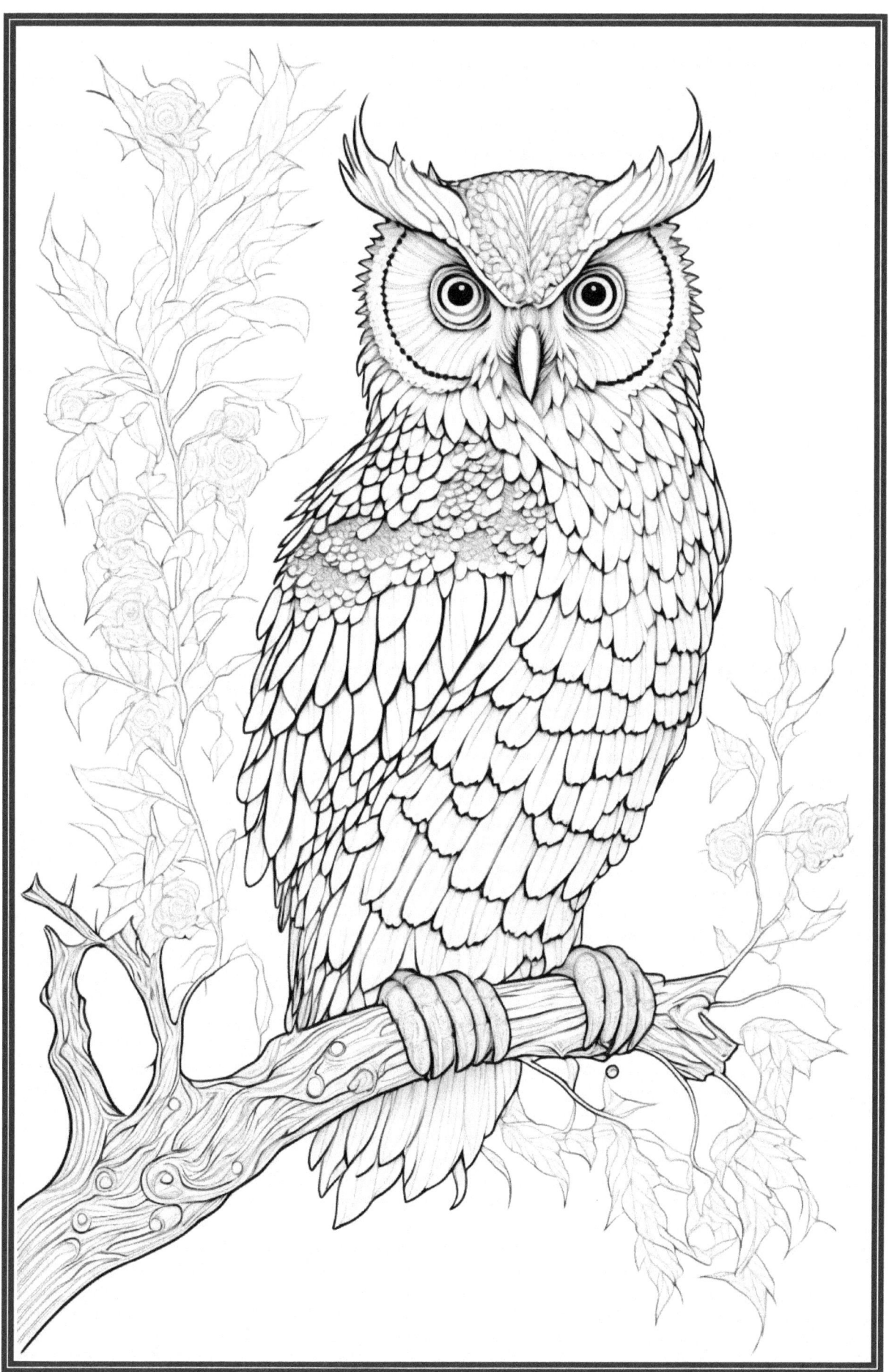

Owls have sharp talons that they use to catch and kill their prey.

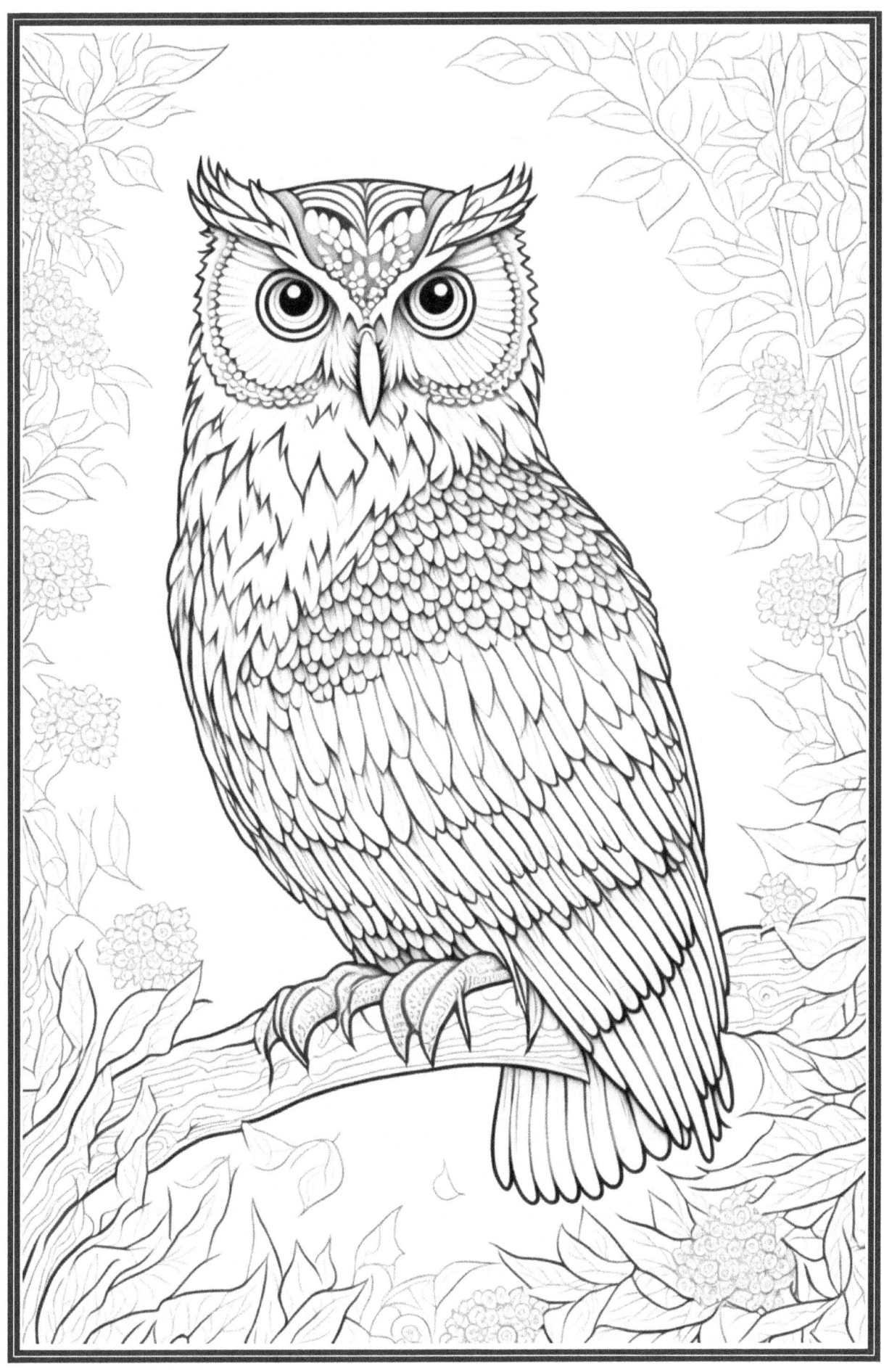

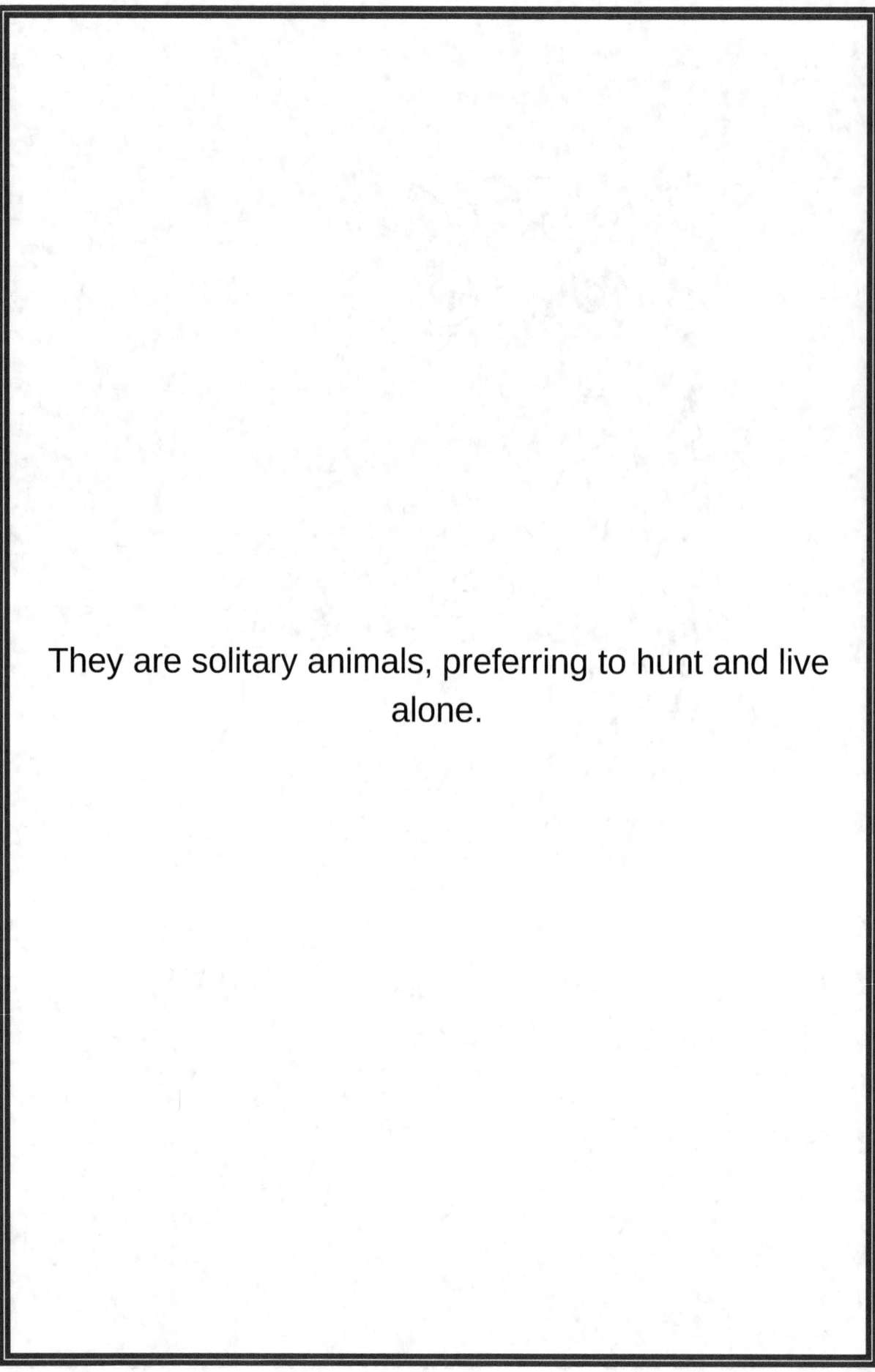

They are solitary animals, preferring to hunt and live alone.

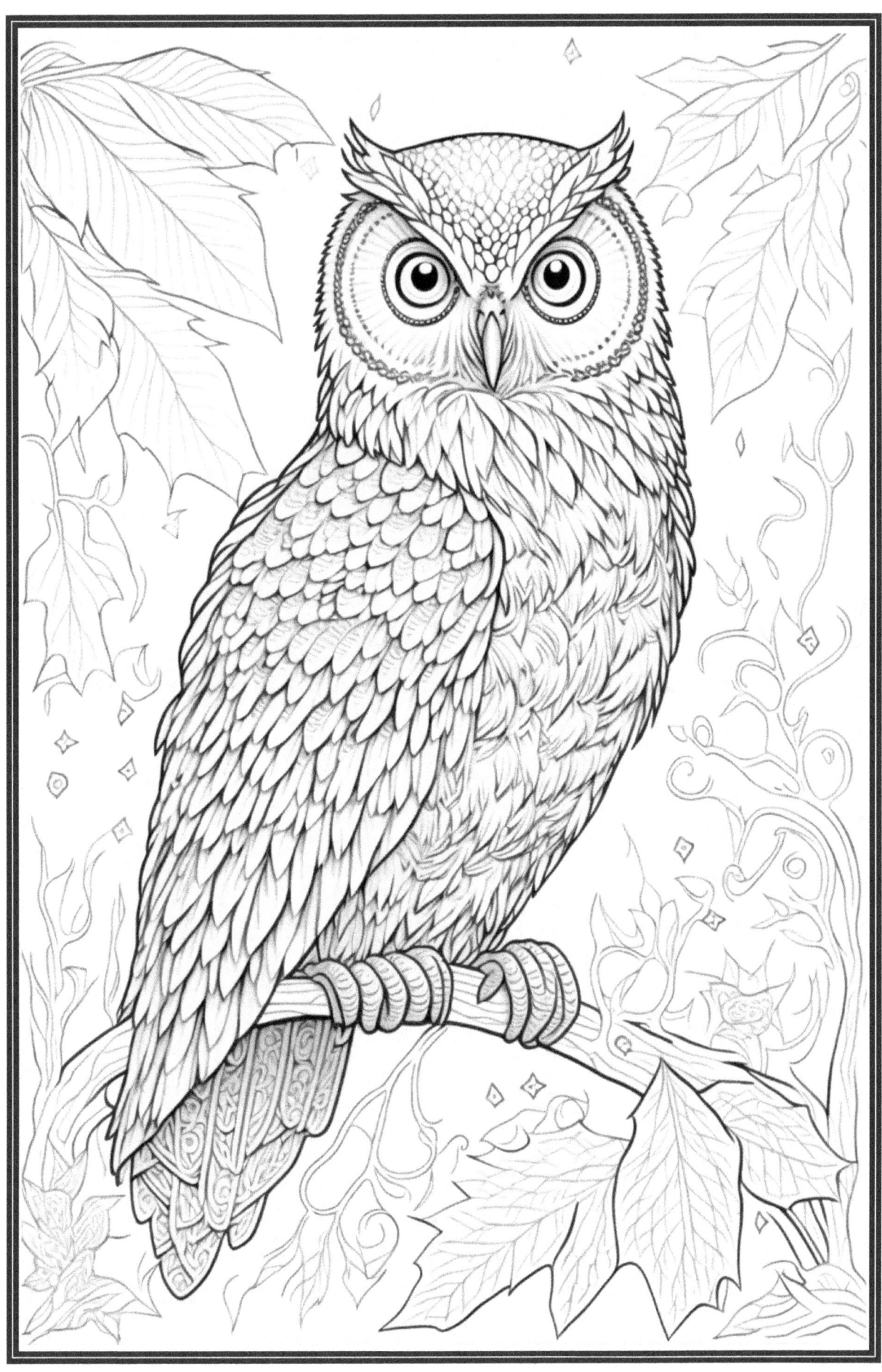

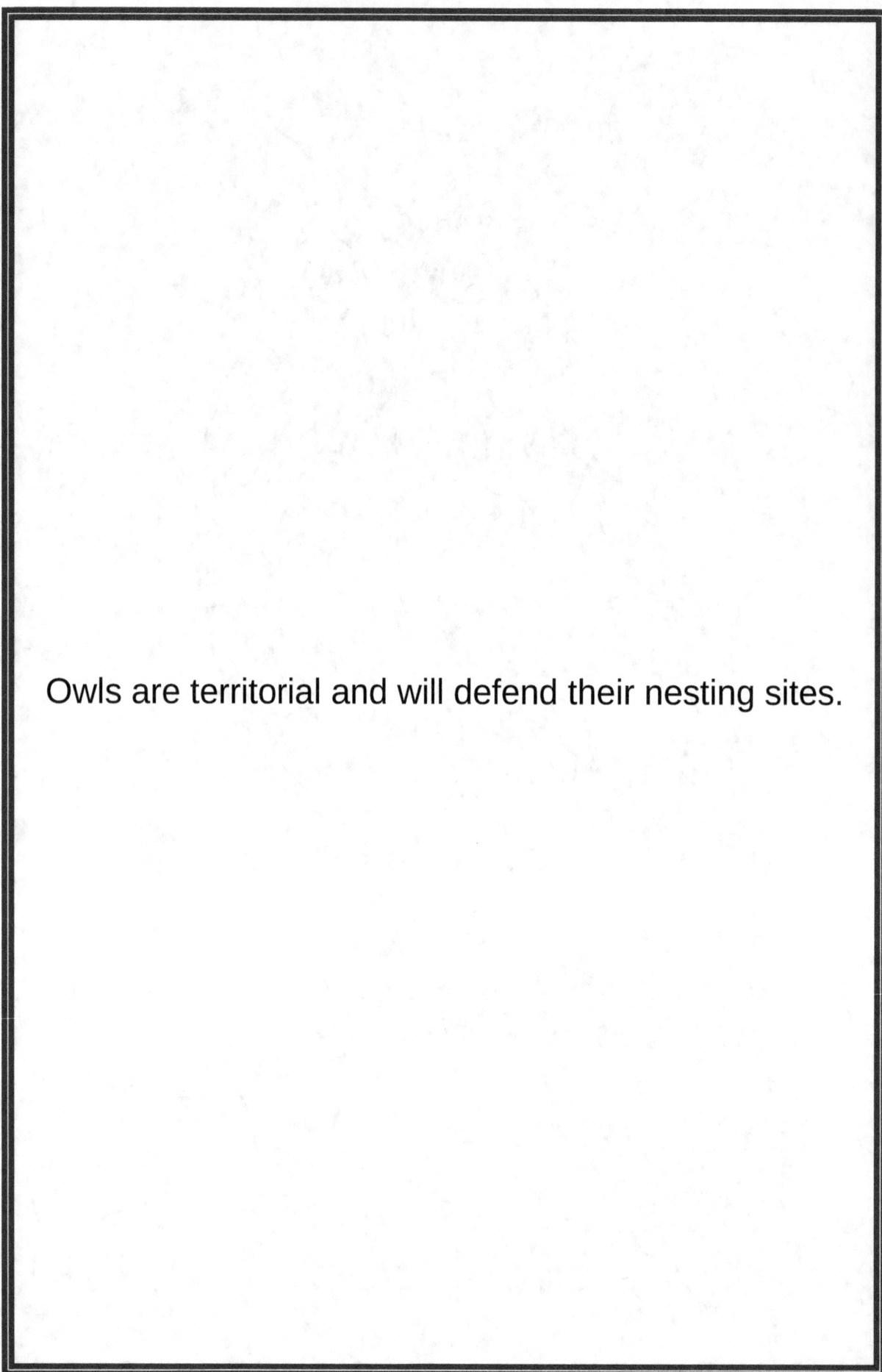

Owls are territorial and will defend their nesting sites.

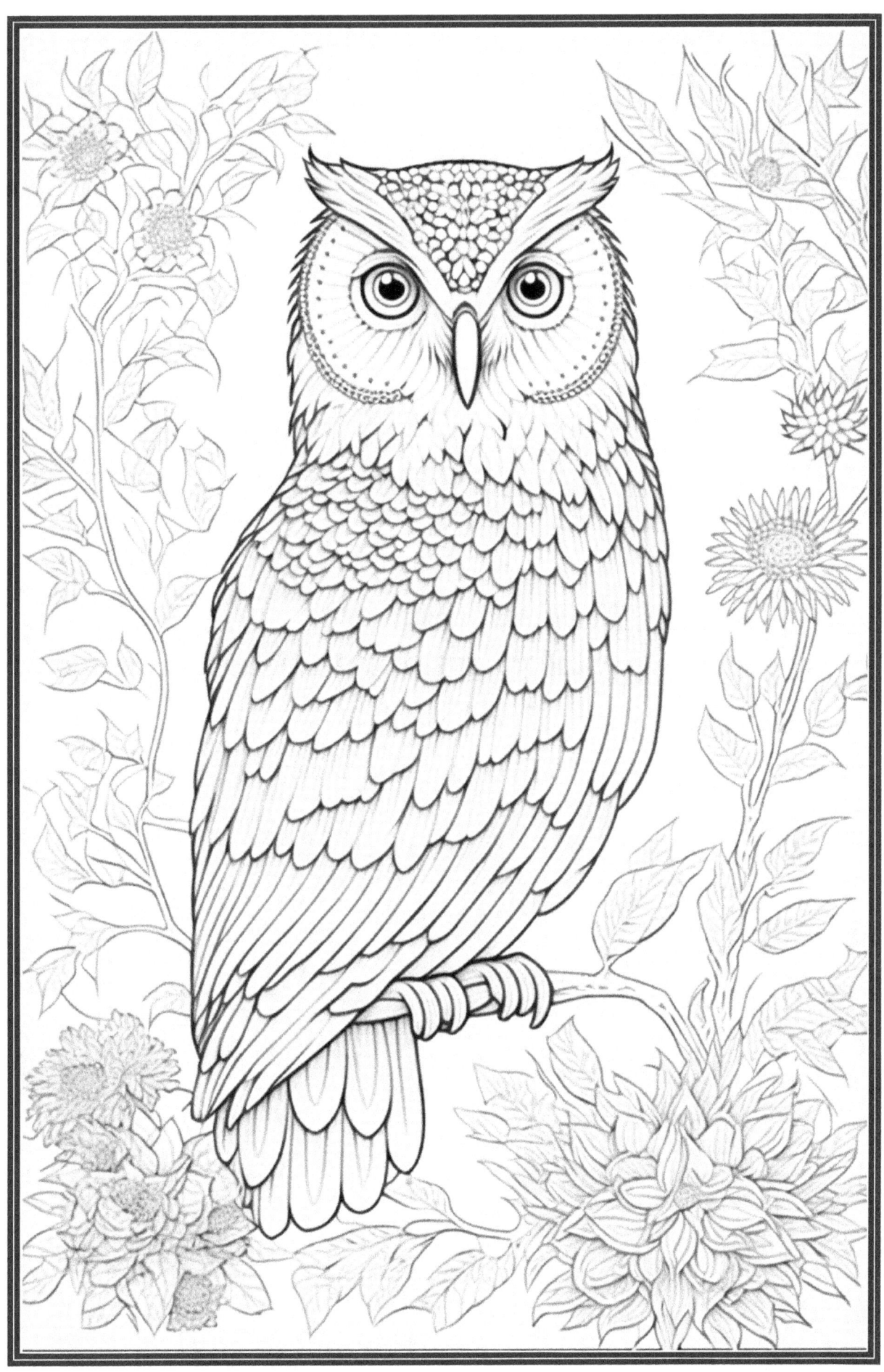

They have a silent flight due to the unique structure of their feathers.

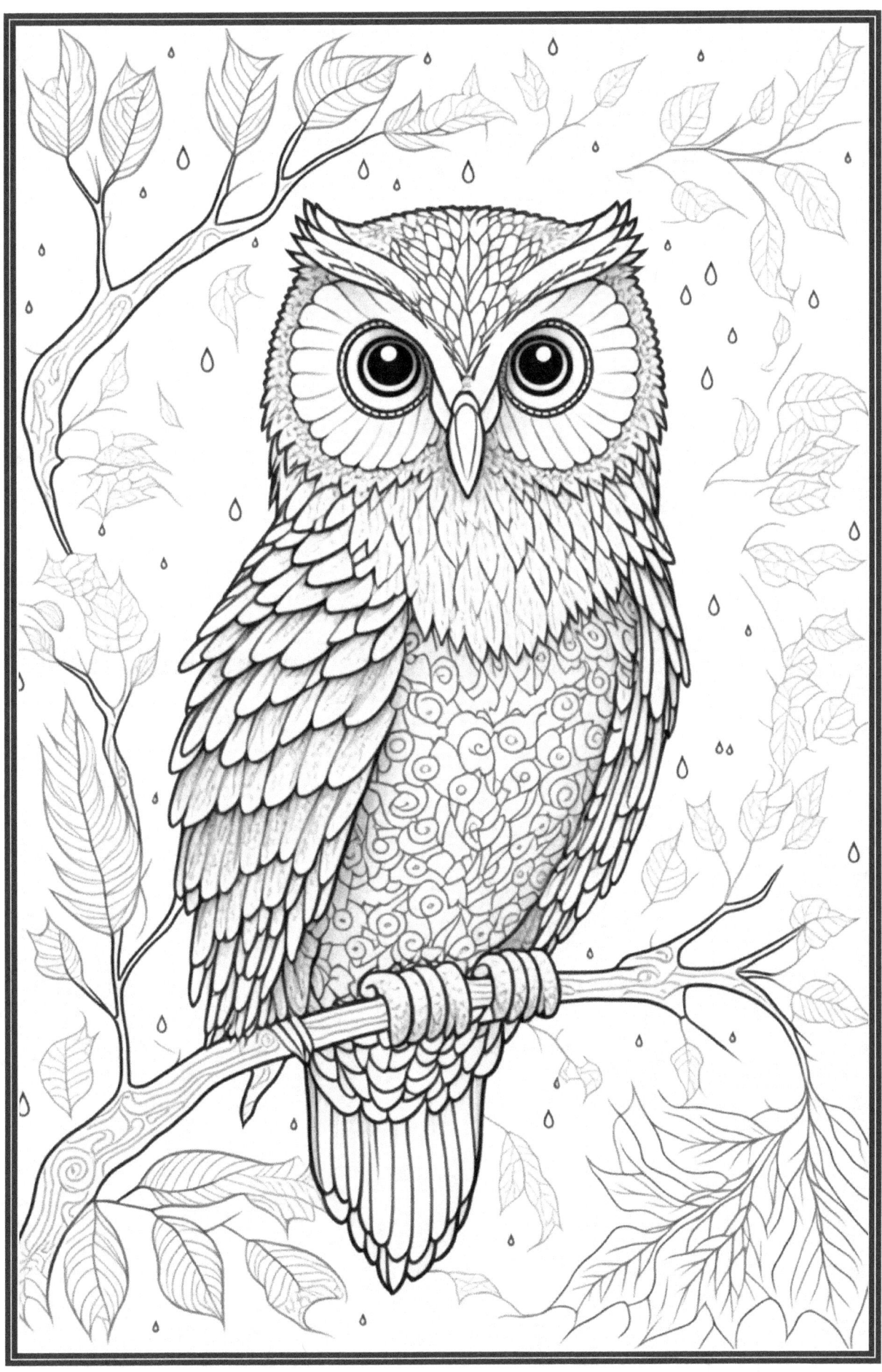

Owls are often associated with wisdom and knowledge in many cultures.

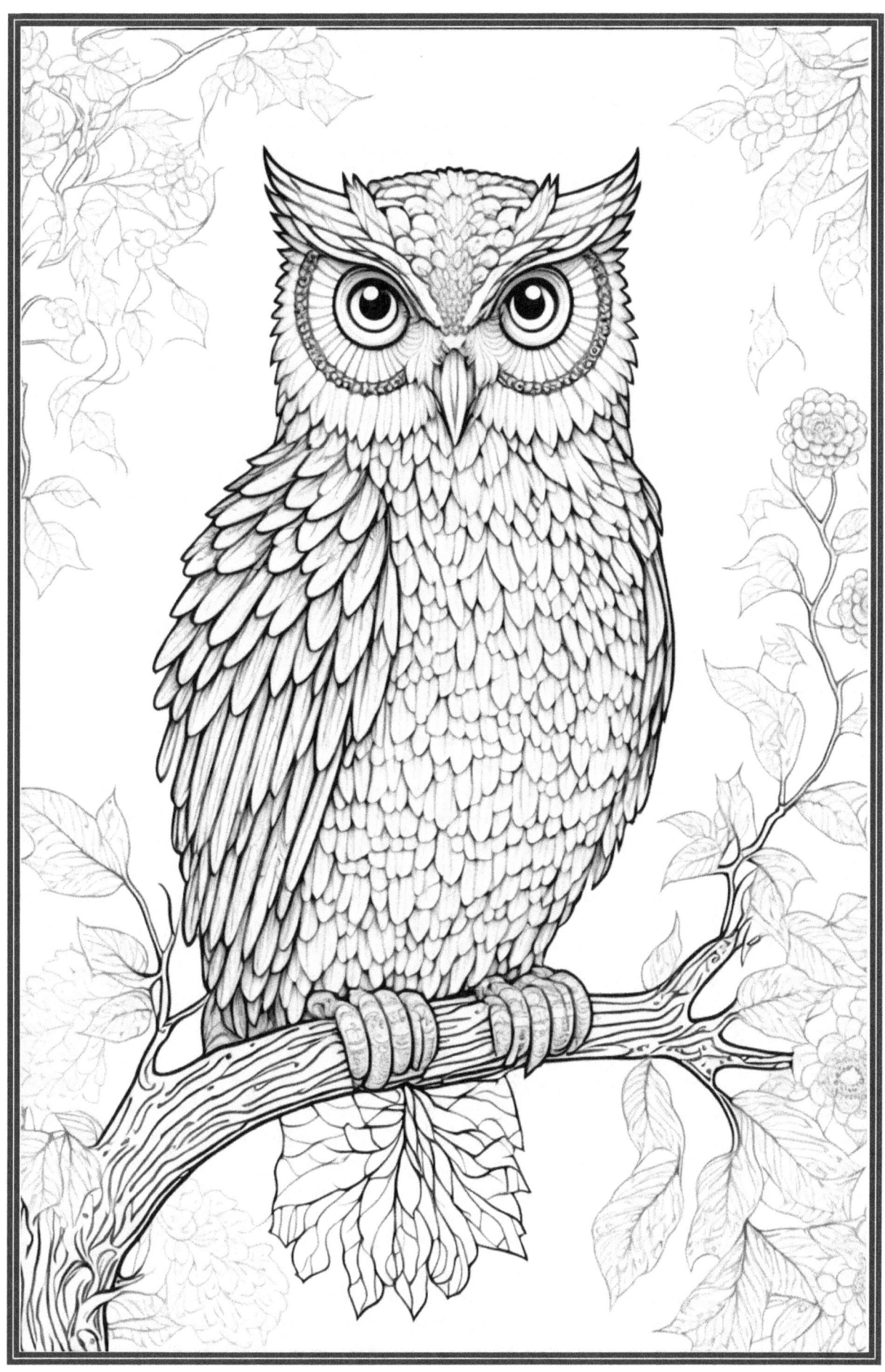

The smallest owl in the world is the elf owl, which is about the size of a sparrow.

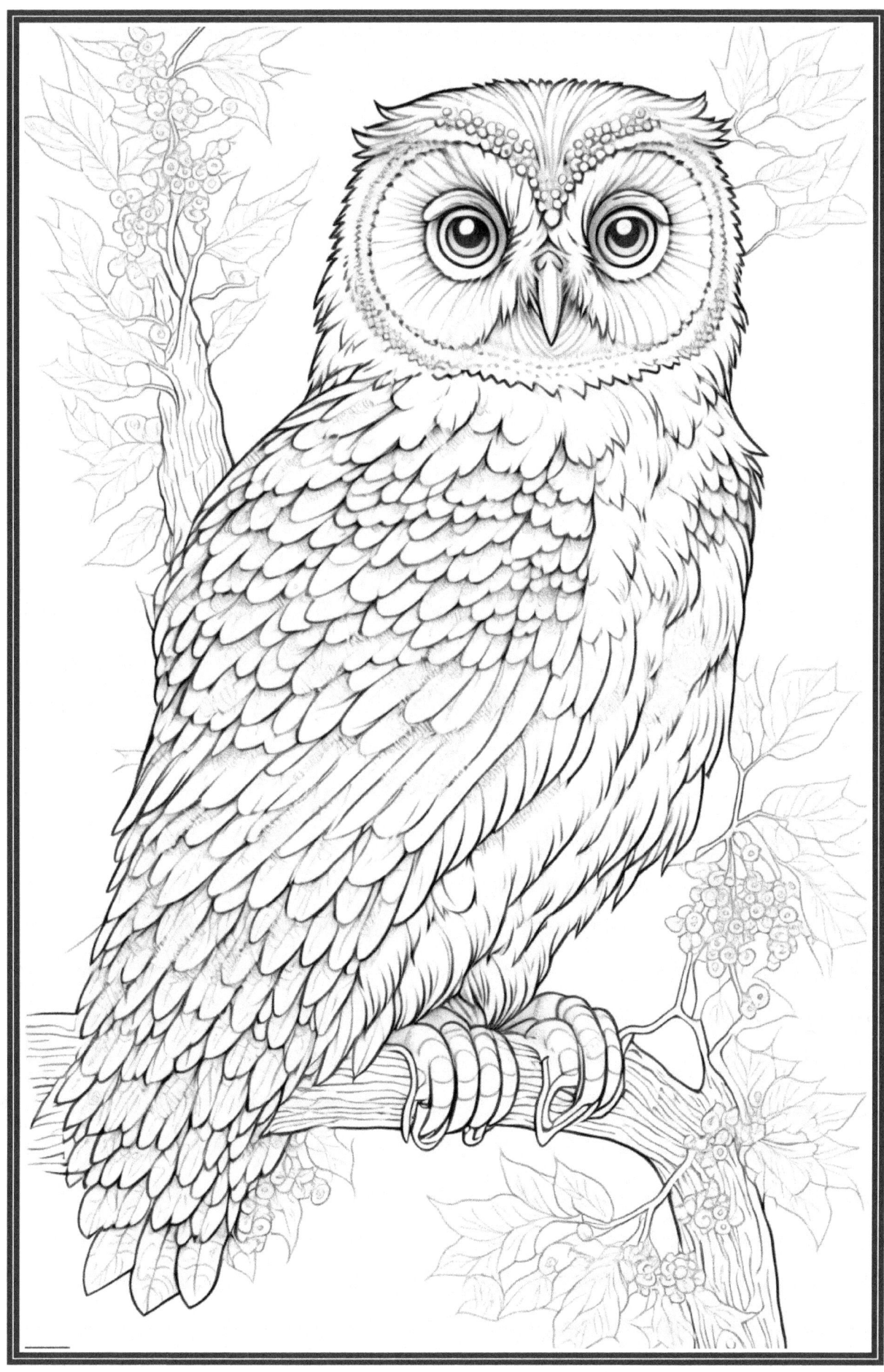

The largest owl in the world is the Eurasian eagle owl, which can have a wingspan of over 6 feet.

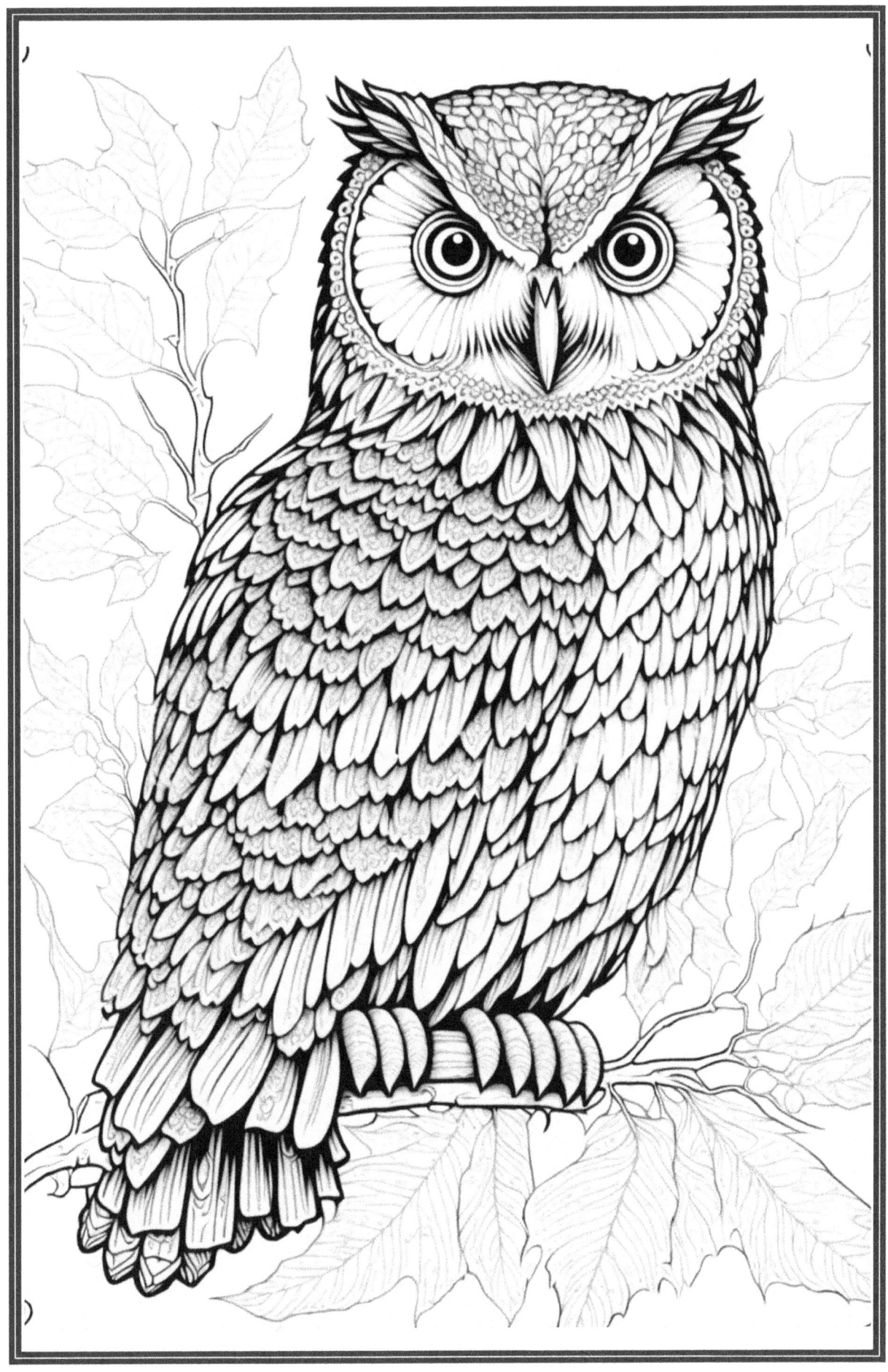

Owls are carnivorous and primarily eat small mammals, birds, and insects.

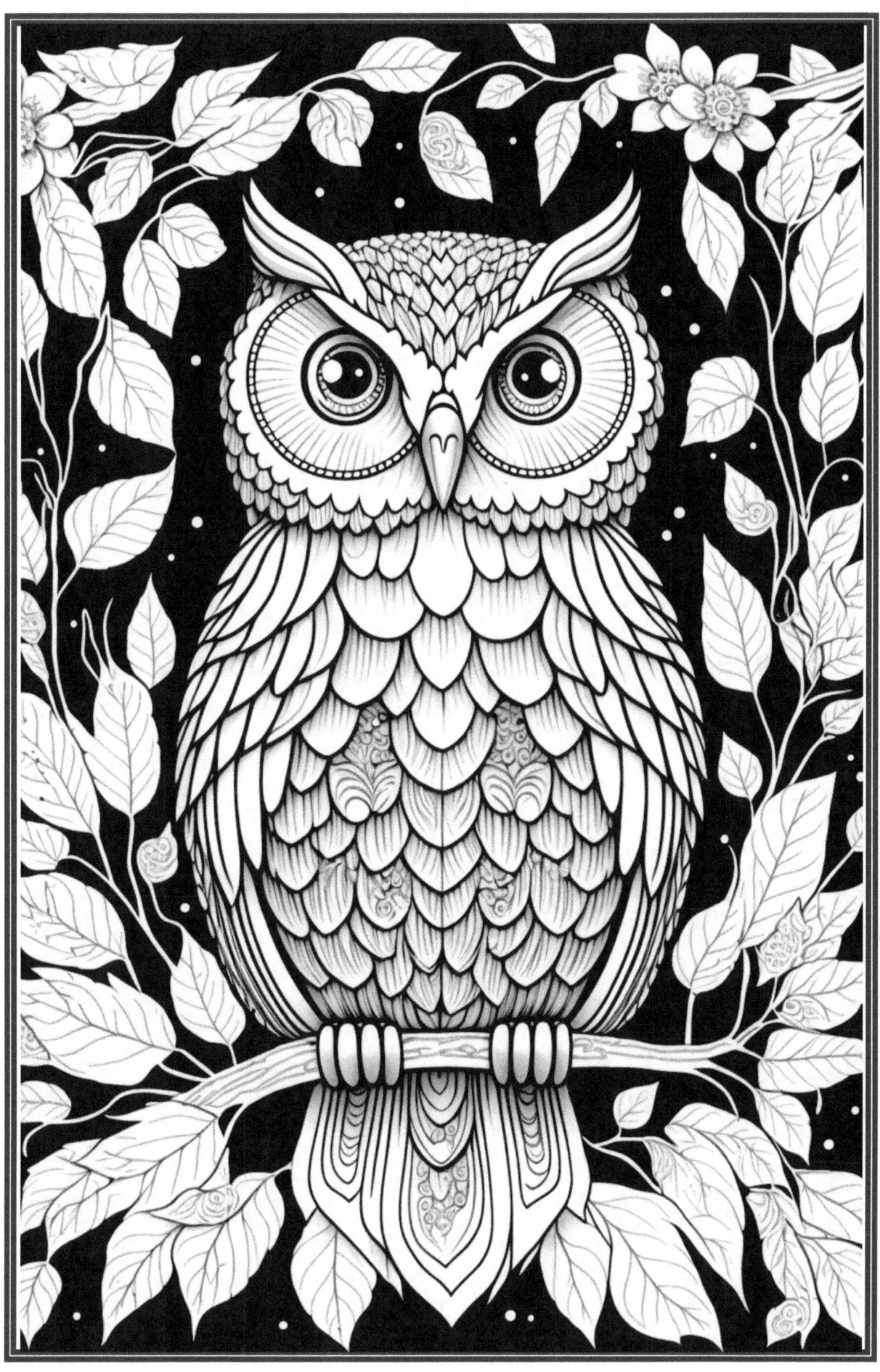

They regurgitate pellets of undigested food, such as bones and fur.

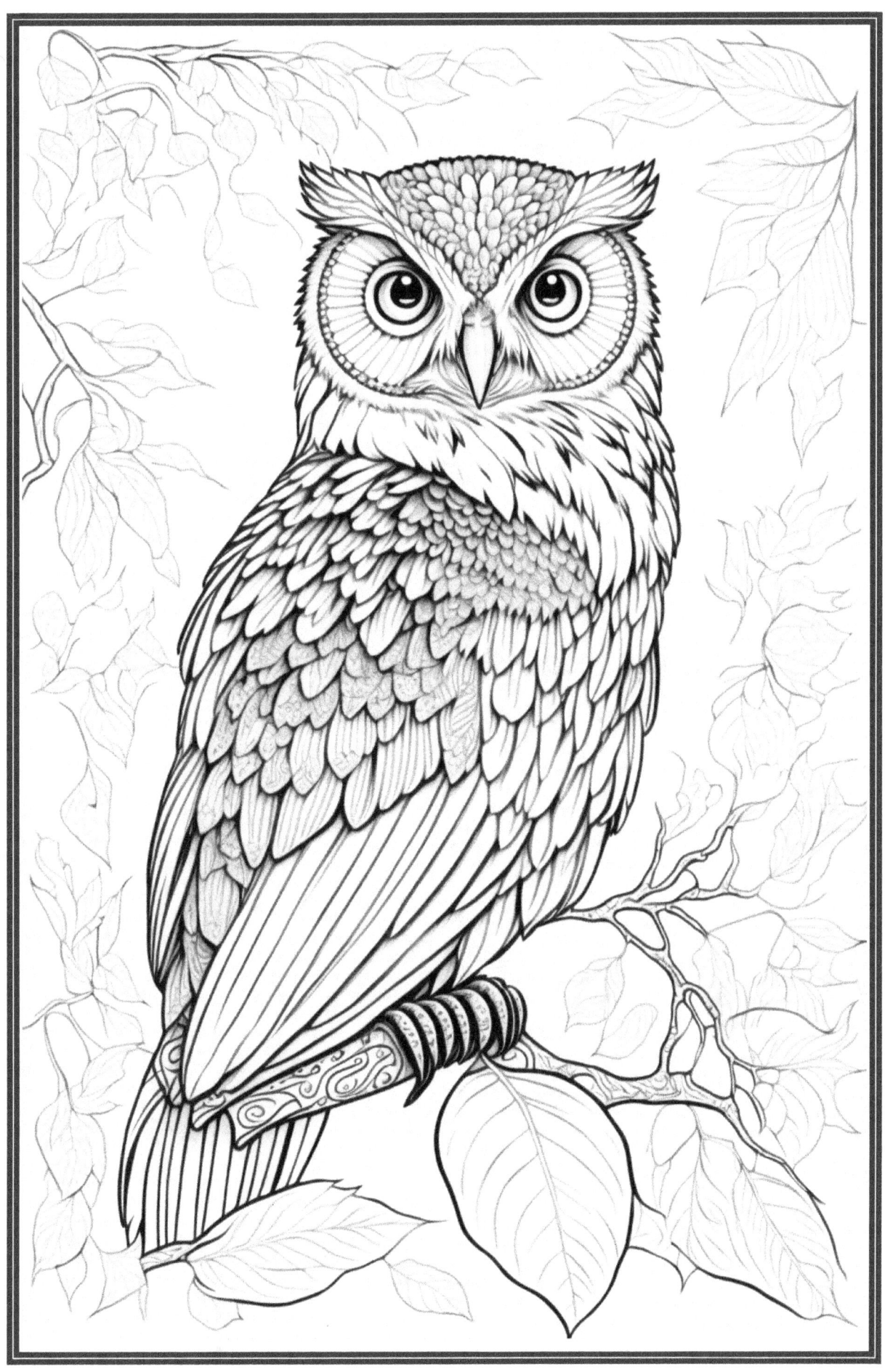

Owls have zygodactyl feet, which means two toes point forward and two points backward.

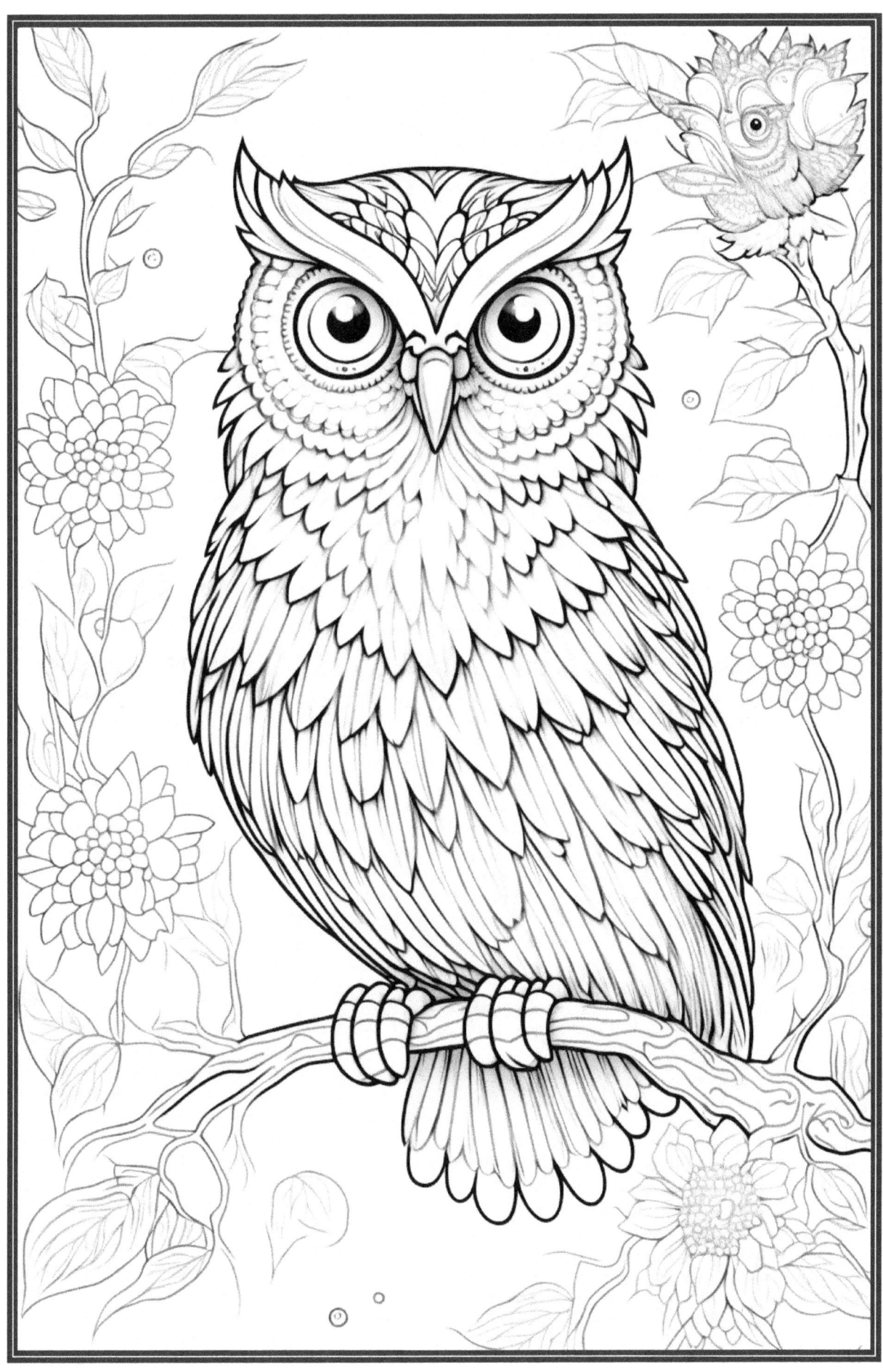

They have a third eyelid called a nictitating membrane, which helps to protect and moisten their eyes.

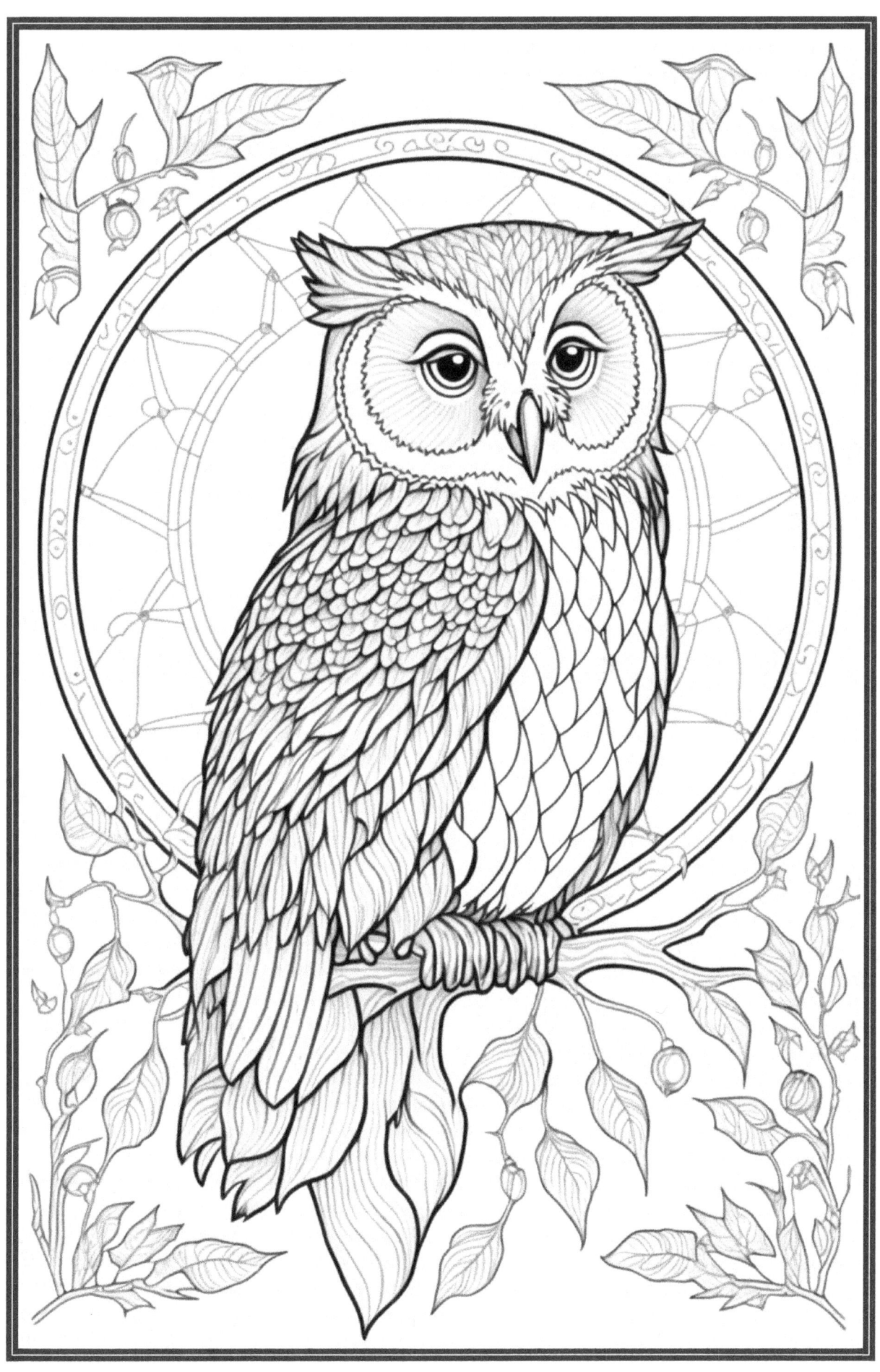

Owls can fly silently due to the specialized edges on their wings.

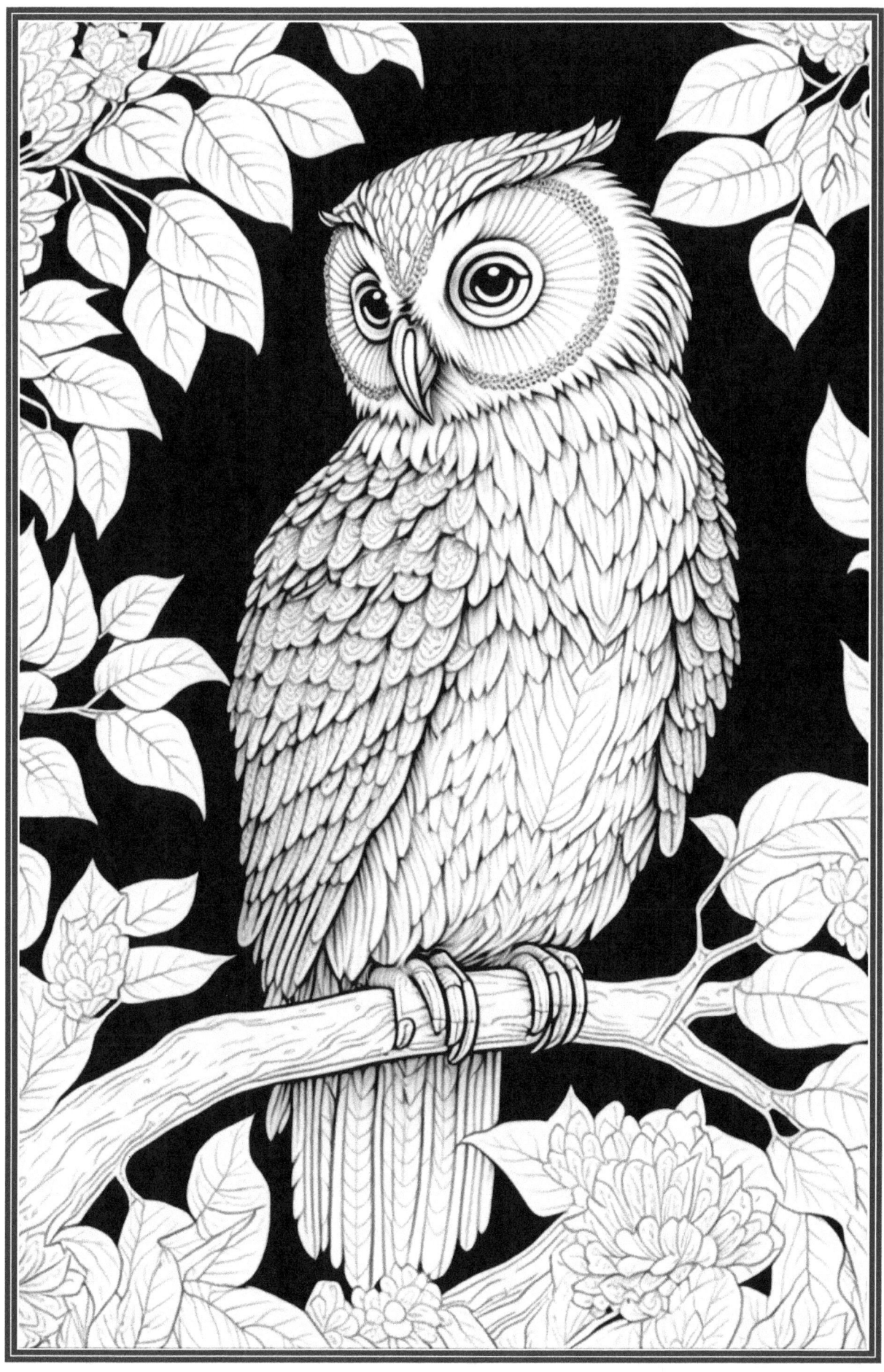

Owls are monogamous and mate for life.

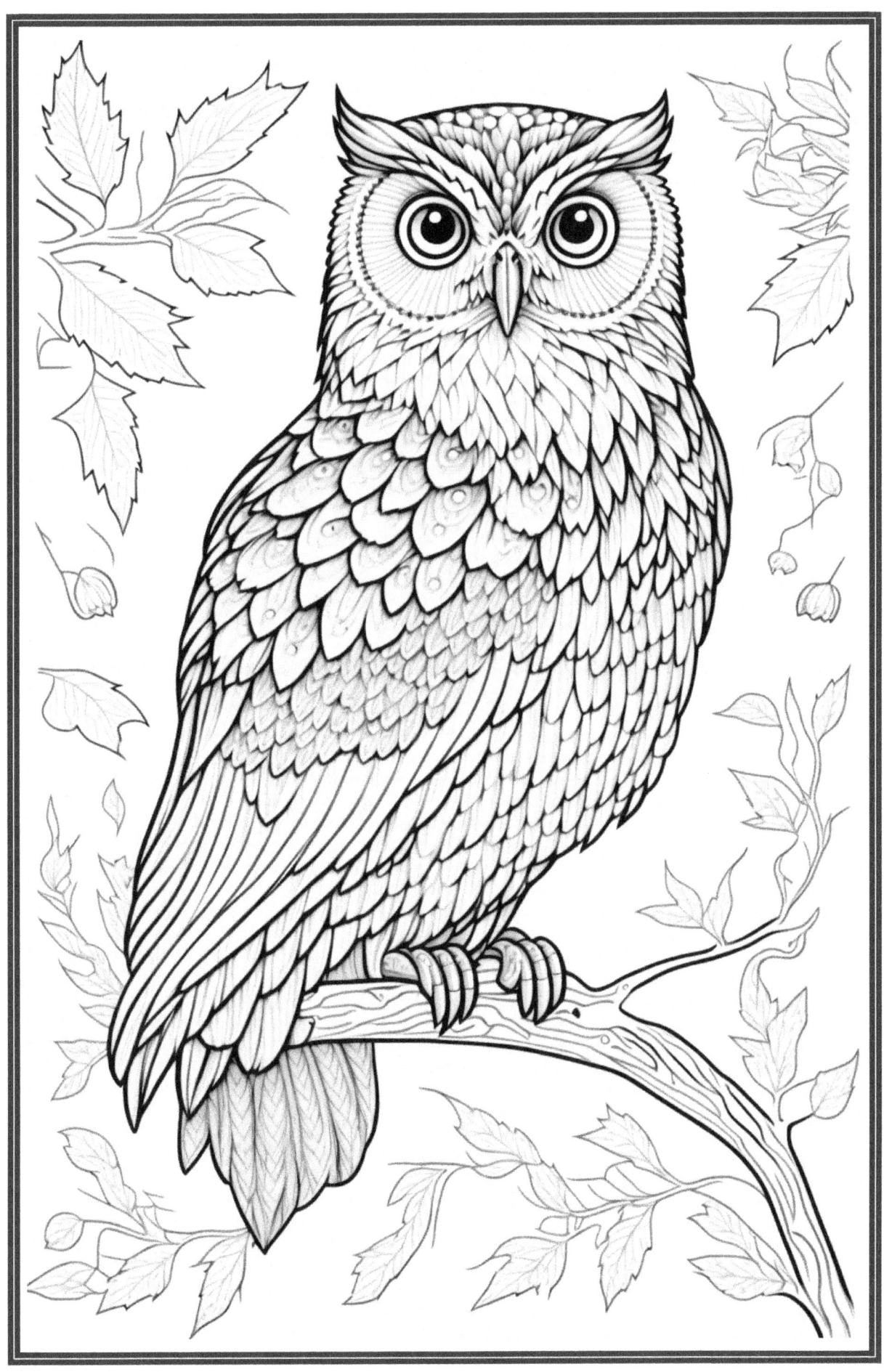

They lay eggs in nests made of twigs, leaves, and other materials.

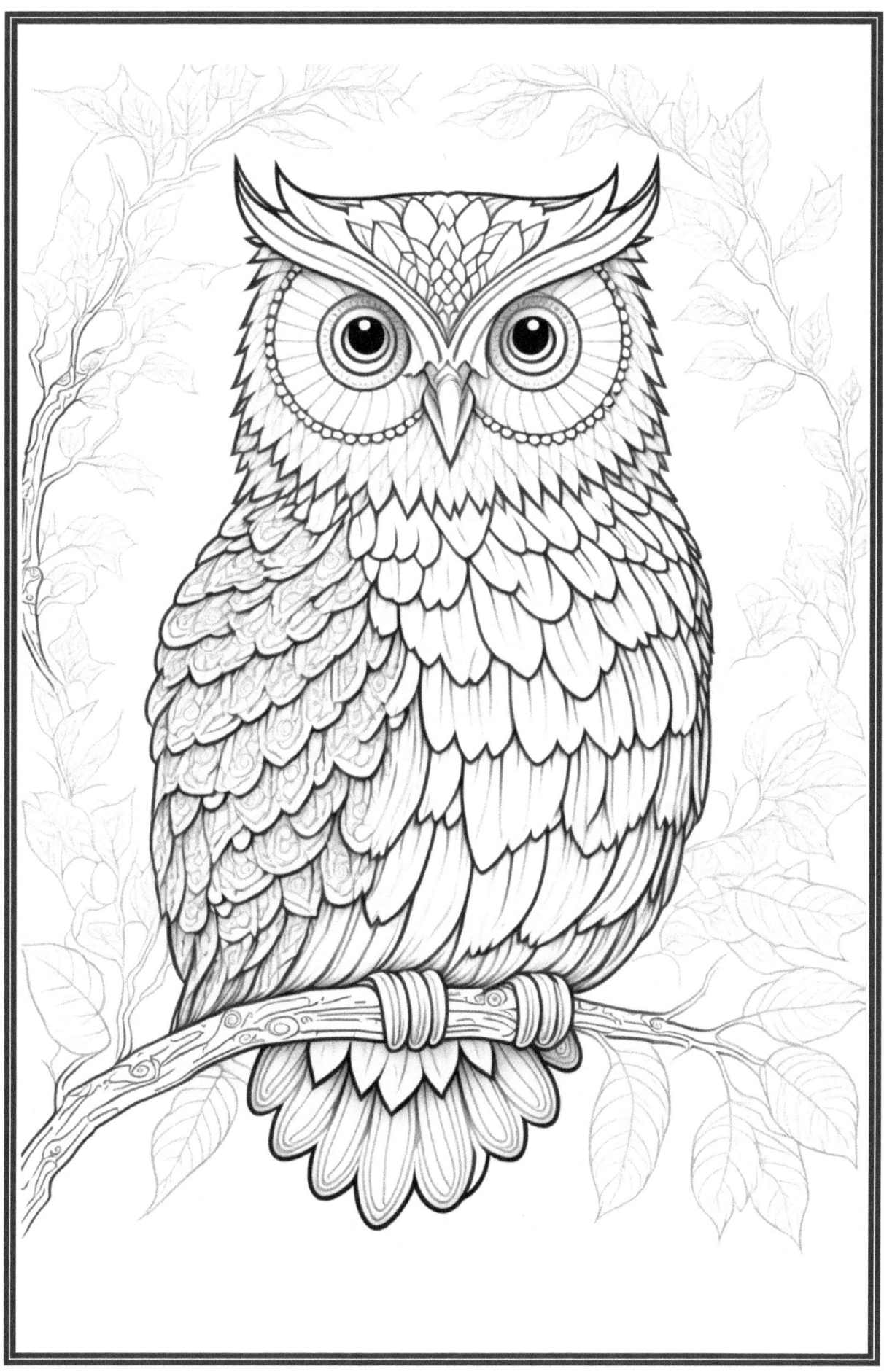

Owls have been known to use abandoned nests of other birds.

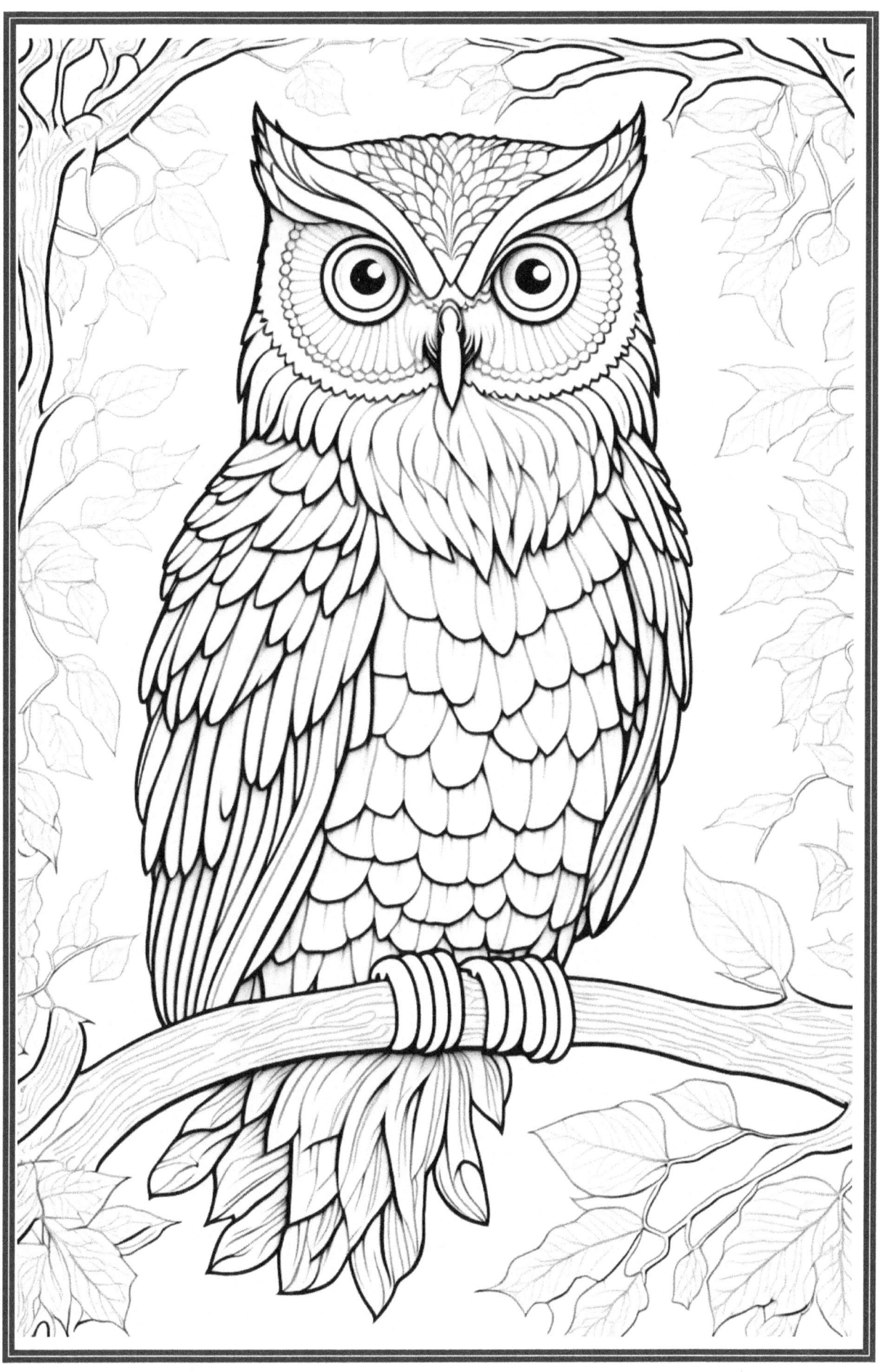

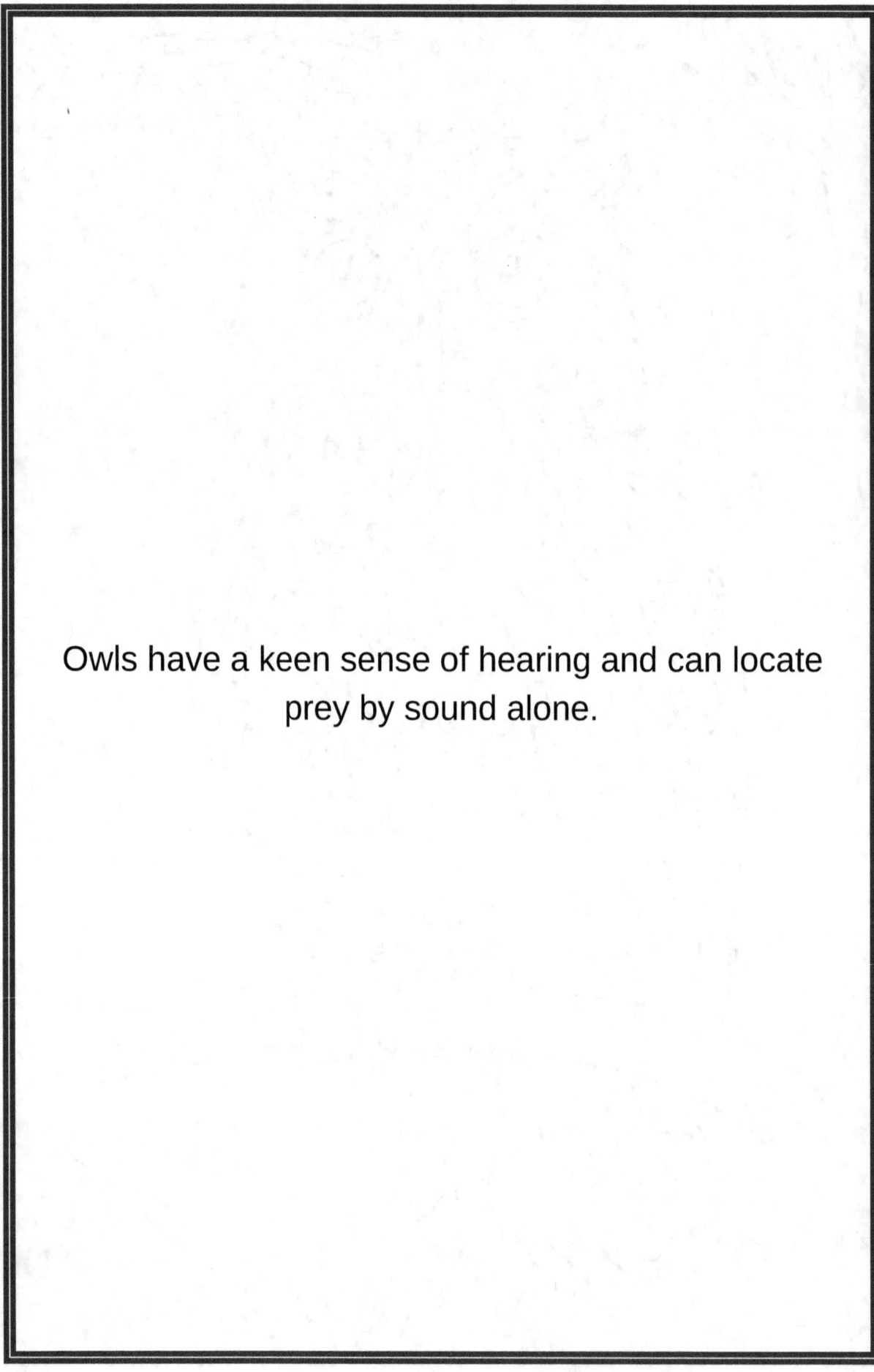

Owls have a keen sense of hearing and can locate prey by sound alone.

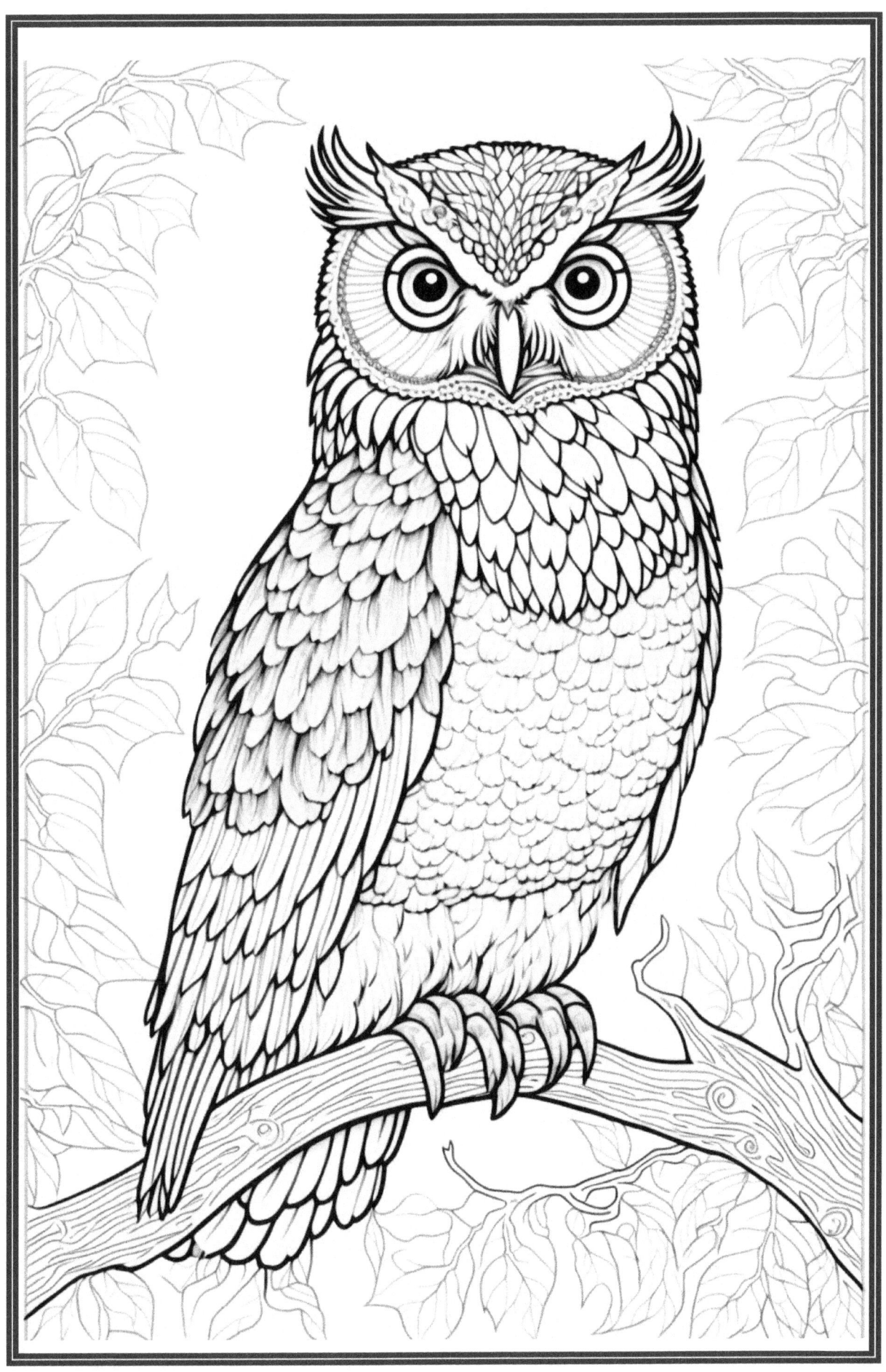

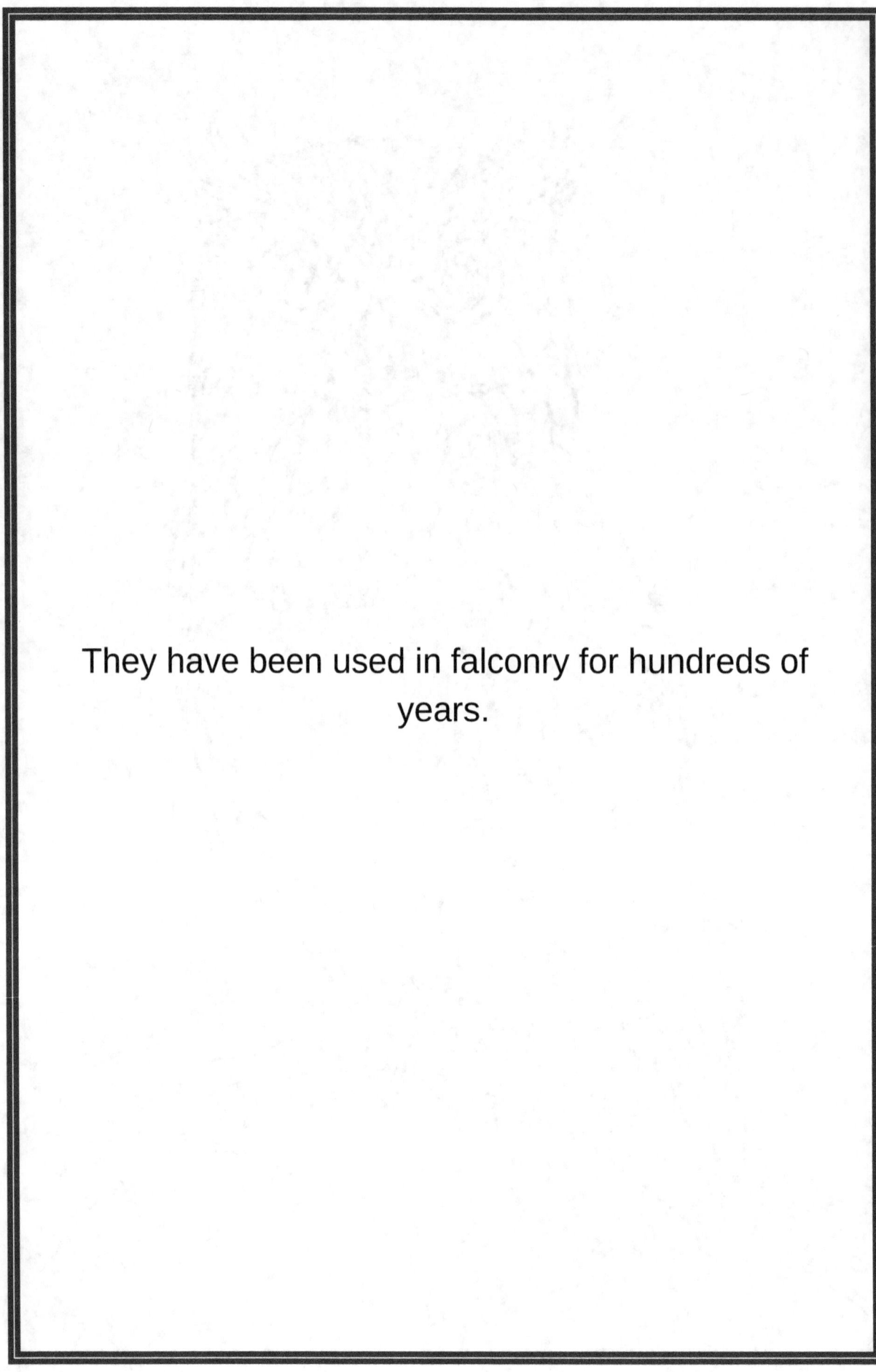

They have been used in falconry for hundreds of years.

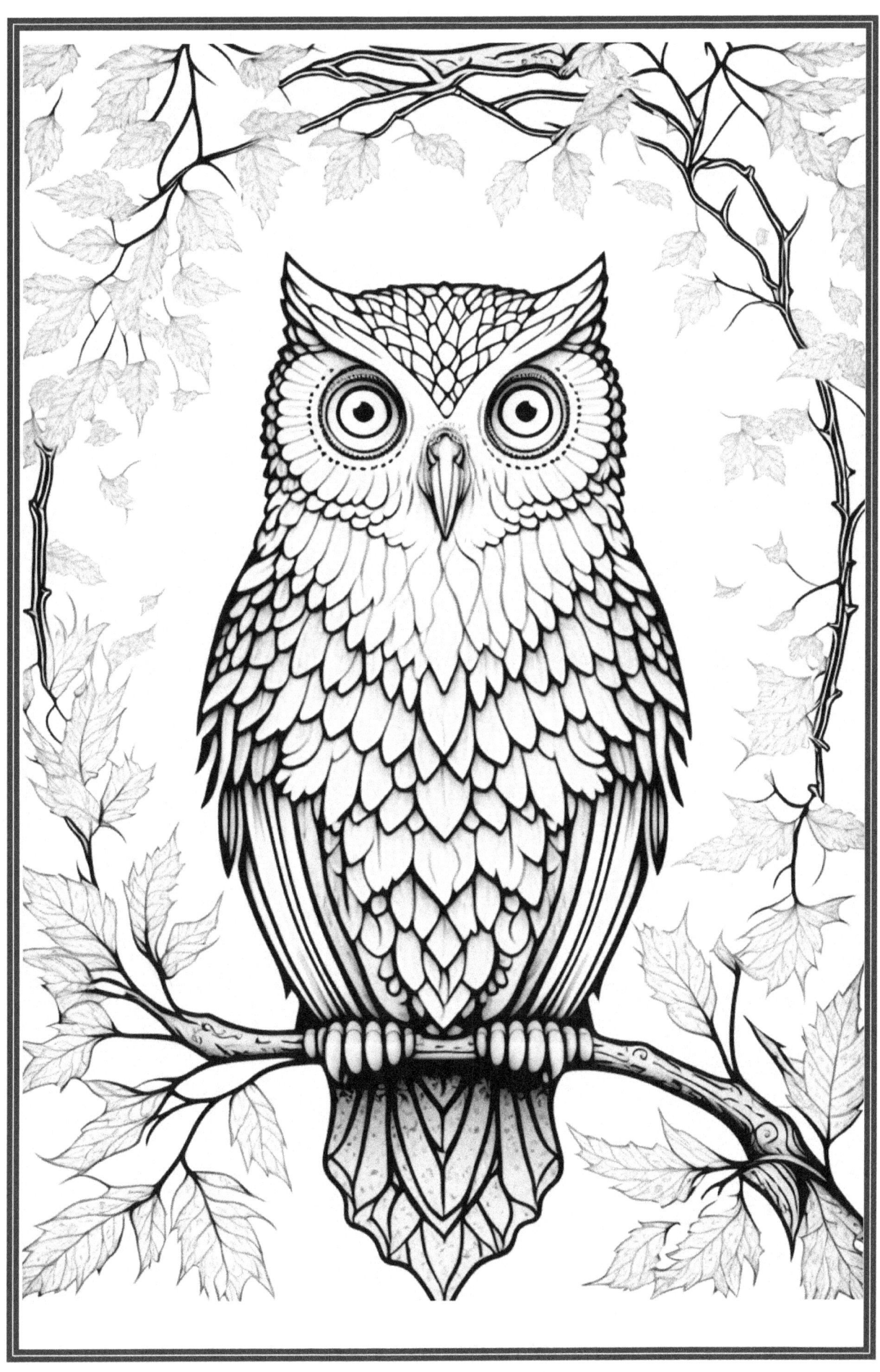

Owls are often depicted in art, literature, and mythology.

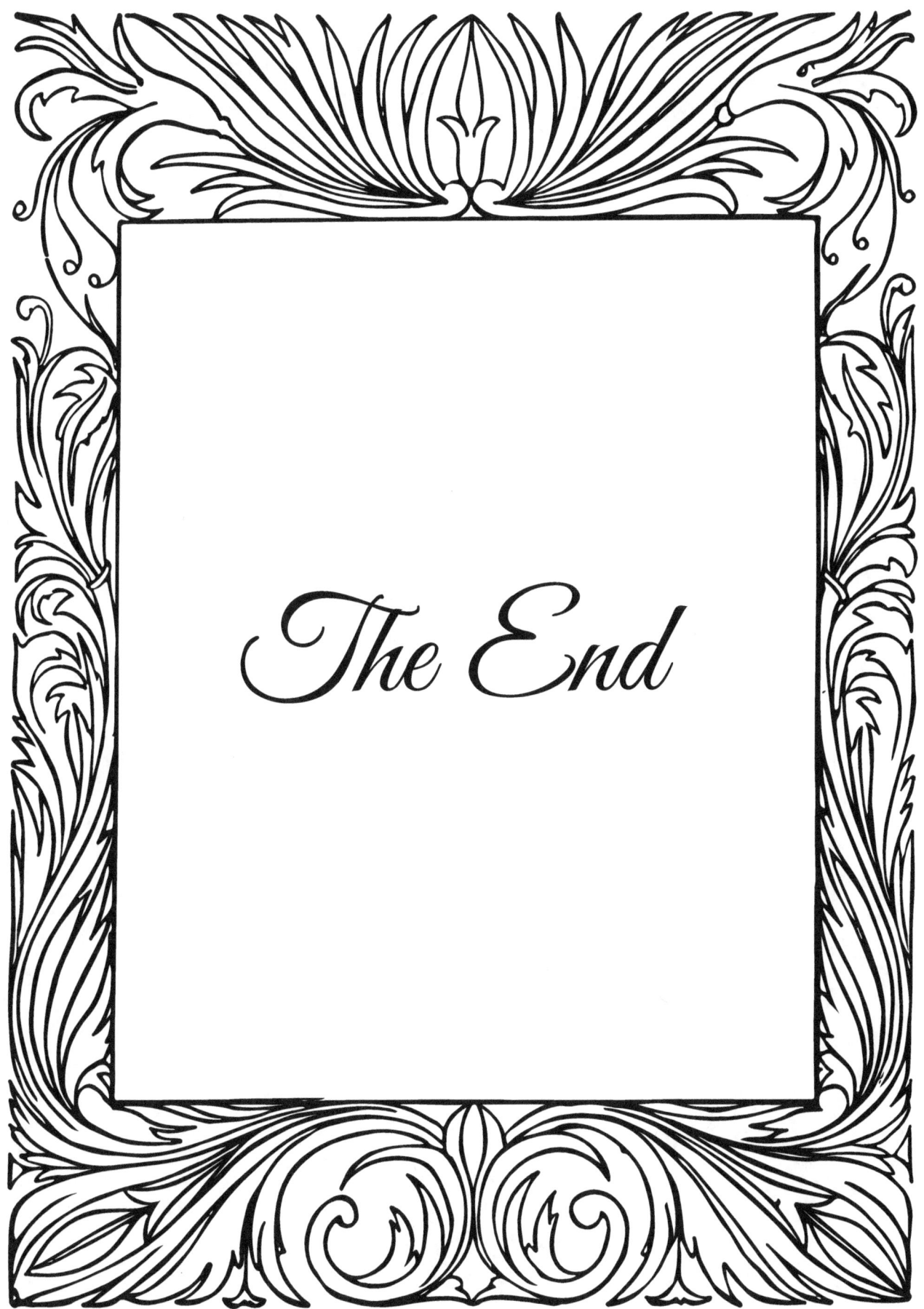

The End